ANGELS AND SUPERNATURAL ENTITIES

DAVE EMMONS

HANGAR 1 PUBLISHING

CONTENTS

Introduction   v

1. Who are these Spiritual Entities?   1
2. What is an Angel?   6
3. What do Angels look like?   9
4. God Directs angels to guard and Protect Us   13
5. Spirit Guides   16
6. Are Angels Male or Female? What are the Bible Facts?   20
7. Angels Interpreted By Other Religions   27
8. Watchers   39
9. Nephilim (Biblical People)   44
10. Confucius   51
11. Beliefs of Ancient India   56
12. What does the Bible say about Demons?   61
13. Were Angels involved in Planning our Country in
    the USA?   64
14. Egyptian Angels and Beliefs   82
15. Do the Nephilim Still Live on Earth Underground?   94
16. Spirits, Ghosts, and Angels   106
17. Fairies and Cryptids   113
18. The Shapeshifters   120
19. Extraterrestrials and Angels   133
20. Are Extraterrestrial Aliens Visiting Earth?   140
21. Human Confusion of Extraterrestrials and Angels   154
22. The Real Supernatural Beings We Need to Protect
    Against   163
23. Human Powers and Abilities   172
24. Actual Experiences with Angels or Extraterrestrials   176
25. Personal and Family Sightings of Real Angels   187
26. Signs That Ghosts or Spirits have visited you   199
27. Signs You're Being Visited by Your Guardian Angel   204
28. Humans Are Supernatural Beings   211

Conclusion   215
About the Author   219
Afterword   221

INTRODUCTION

I have been told that Angels are a tricky topic to cover. I will stay within the historical and Biblical context. I am inserting my personal experiences and other accounts of people experiencing Angelic intervention. This is a topic I have wanted to write about since my publishing first two books. In my first book, I speak about very unusual events that broadened my consciousness and renewed my faith that there is life after physical death – a much better life. In my second book, I write about my Vietnam Combat memoirs and why wars are senseless. These experiences have prepared me to feel that God exists and is within us for infinity. I have gotten a preview of the other side: Jesus Christ called many mansions in Heaven; what science knows now is that he might have meant many dimensional levels.

Do Angels and Watchers have the same spiritual powers to intervene in our lives, redirect our path, or perform miracles? In my research and in this book, I hope to give some answers to that question. Watchers were mentioned in the Bible numerous times. Watchers also alerted Jesus when the Roman Soldiers were close by, especially when he was at a friend's house for a meal and worship. Who were these, Watchers? We will explore the Bible and credible archeological records to find out what we can of the truth about Watchers.

I want to discuss Guides briefly and earthly Custodians and where they fit into the scheme of spiritual order here on our planet. Guides are mentioned by the American Native Indians as their spiritual masters. My experiences with Native American Indian Guides were an eye-opener as a Spiritual person and accurately described my future spiritual journey. In our past and present times, you hear people talk of Custodians of our earth. Could all these spiritual beings be the same as Angels or something else? Custodians clean up our spiritual energies and keep the order of our planet. I suspect Custodians work with everyone's spiritual needs since we need spiritual support for our souls in times of need.

Since I have a book on life on other planets, I will try to explain that they are God's creations too, just like us. The ancient civilizations called other life forms gods, but we know they were not gods. Only one God has created all the universes and is a mighty consciousness that flows through our souls and minds. I always say "God of gods" to define the divinity – God.

Is it possible that not all Angels and Watchers are good to us humans? Or are there entities that don't have our best interest in their work on earth? As mentioned in the Bible, some demons always await an opportunity to invade our souls. As we can see today, some evil people don't have any respect for life. They seem to be taken over by hostile powers to cause indescribable pain and destruction to their fellow humans. Mostly in the name of greed and self-fulfilling enrichment.

In this book, you will find other supernatural beings discussed that are not angels but are supernatural forces that visit our earthly realm. I write about these entities to compare real angels to beings that can mimic angels' characteristics. Most of these entities discussed come from other dimensions or universes, as angels do. Traveling thousands of light years to reach Earth is not a problem because time and space for angels and other supernatural beings are limitless. These and other questions about the supernatural are explained in this book. There are so many theories and opinions from experts about this subject, but none of us have accurate answers. Maybe I can make sense of this dilemma with my research and ideas based on my real-life experiences.

This book is different from other angel and watchers' books because it covers almost all supernatural beings from ancient Biblical times to the modern day. Some of the mysterious beings, like Nephilim Giants, Dragons, Big Foot, Fairies, Cryptids, and the serpent in the Garden of Eden. We had less knowledge of creatures in ancient times because there were no pictures or texts to describe these creatures. Sure, there are stone sculptures and cave drawings we can try to decipher, but there is evidence that is lacking. This book explores the relationship between ancient times and modern-day pictures and witnesses. In the Bible, some people and Prophets witnessed angels and alien-type beings. I make Biblical references to these events to keep the accuracy of the Bible's authenticity in proper perspective.

What makes this book different is that it is refreshing to have numerous topics and titles to discuss other than one or two entities being the focus. Every topic in this book is a mystery, from ghosts to extraterrestrial aliens. I hope you discover some understanding of some of the questions you have about angels and all supernatural mysteries. I start the book by describing almost all religious types of angels – Angels 101, I call it. Then I move on to the other mysterious questions and entities in our history and today's news announcements of strange events.

WHO ARE THESE SPIRITUAL ENTITIES?

Who, or what, are these Angels? According to the Bible, Angels are messengers of God, and he communicates through angels for humans to hear God's word or receive God's help. We can also speak directly to God through prayer and meditation.

There are a variety of angels, each with a distinct purpose and duty. (HowStuffWorks) There are three major groups of angels known as choirs. This is where the religions get their name for singing choirs that sing gospel music in Churches. Ancient texts also say there are nine types of angels. No matter where these angels are in the hierarchy, just like us, they are individuals.

Angels can see far beyond our mortal timeline and know our destinies. They have the characteristics God has instilled in them, like being extremely patient, forgiving, kind, and mostly showing love. Angels are always aware of our personal goals, and God assigns them to assist us. They will never interfere with our free will. God makes that rule of not interfering in our free will for humans and other lifeforms in the universe. God is more significant than our definition can define them as being. God is the almighty consciousness of the many universes that gives light and life to all life forms.

There are nine types of angels spoken about in the Bible and ancient texts. I will list them and briefly describe them. (HowStuffWorks)

1. Seraphim

Seraphim means the fiery ones. The Bible mentions these angels as having faces, hands, and feet. Each one has six wings, and they use four wings to cover themselves in the presence of God as a sign of humility. They are depicted in religious art. Seraphim is the plural of the word "seraph." They also appear to worship God continuously.

2. Cherubim (Plural of Cherub)

These angels are the closest to God, encircle his throne, and emit an intense, fiery light representing love. They are considered fiery serpents. Not even other divine beings can look at them. There are only four Cherubs, each having four faces and six wings. When they visit Earth, they leave their serpent appearance behind. These angels prefer tall, thin, clean-cut human embodiments to blend in with humans.

3. Thrones

These angels are the keepers of celestial records and hold the knowledge of God. They are sent to Earth with great tasks. Their first task was expelling humankind from the Garden of Eden. Thrones have the most bizarre appearance. They look like great glowing wheels covered with many eyes.

4. Dominions

These dominion angels are considered middle management. They receive orders from seraphim and cherubim, then dish out orders to the "worker bee" angels of lower orders. Their primary purpose is to ensure the cosmos remains orderly by sending down power to heads of government and other authority figures. Zadkiel is the chief of this order.

5. Virtues

Shaped like sparks of light, virtues oversee maintaining the natural world. They inspire living things in areas such as science. They take orders from the angels above and convert them into miracles for the deserving. When making themselves known to us in their earthly form, they are musicians, artists, healers, and scientists.

6. Powers

In celestial form, powers appear like brightly colored, hazy fumes. Powers are border agents between Heaven and Earth. They are the angels of birth and death. Some believe they preside over demons who wish to overthrow the world. St. Paul thought the powers themselves were the evil ones. (HowStuffWorks)

7. Principalities

These angelic beings are shaped like rays of light. As a school principal, it is the principalities that oversee everything. They guide our entire world – nations, cities, and towns. They are also in charge of religion and politics.

8. Archangels

Archangels respond best when dealing with matters involving all humankind. They are the first order of angels that appear only in human form. They function among us as pioneers for change in the form of explorers, philosophers, and human rights leaders. These angels are common because of being mentioned in the Bible – Michael, Gabriel, Raphael, Uriel, Saraqael, Raguel, and Remiel. Seven archangels in total.

9. Angels

These angels are called "regular angels." They are guardians of people and all things physical and are the most common type of angel. They are sent as messengers to humanity by God. Personal guardian angels come from this group of angels. These angels may protect and warn humans and act as warriors on behalf of God. (HowStuffWorks)

As mentioned in Isaiah (Bible) 6:1-7, Seraphim is the most powerful class of angels. They are caretakers of the Almighty's throne.

2

WHAT IS AN ANGEL?

Angels are not plump babies with rosy cheeks with wings. Angels of the Bible are powerful and mighty. (housemixblog.-com) The Greek word "Angelos" means messengers of God. They do God's work (Heb 1:14). On some rare occasions, God addresses an issue himself.

They are spiritual beings not of flesh and blood, though sometimes they appear human (Heb 13:2, Luke 24:39). They are loyal to the Lord, worshiping him endlessly (Psalm 103, Rev 7). They have a will, intellect, and emotion (Jude 1:6). Angels are glorious beings, but they are not to be worshipped or prayed to.

Angels declare themselves as fellow servants of humans, and they come to Earth to assist humans. God has appointed angels to help humans when possible. Some events in a human's life direction are supposed to happen, and they can't change your destiny. The heavenly workers of God highly respect a human's free will. John (of the Bible) fell to his feet to worship an angel. The angel said to John, "Don't do that! I am a fellow servant with you and your brothers and sisters who hold to the testimony of Jesus. Worship God!" (Rev 19:10)

For he will command his angels concerning you to guard you in all ways. (PSALM 91:11) (Housemixblog.com)

Angels are created beings; they have not always existed (Neh 9:6). They were created through Christ for Christ (Col 1:16). The Bible says they were created before the Earth was formed. They shouted for joy! (Job 38:7) There had to be different groups of angels created to serve the human spirit's needs. The latter statement that angels were created when the Earth was formed seems that the angels had varying duties. God had his angels long before humans inhabited Earth. They might have had otherworldly duties throughout God's creation in the universes. Then when Christ ascended to Heaven, God created the nine angels earlier described.

The question of, how many angels are there? We don't know the exact number, but that the number is "innumerable" (Heb 12:22). Daniel said about God on the throne, "a thousand thousands," served him, and ten thousand times ten thousand stood before God; the court sat in judgment, and the books were open." That is 100 million angels right there! Then I looked, and I heard around the throne and the living creatures and the elders with the voice of many angels, numbering myriads and thousands of thousands. (Revelations 5:11)

Other definitions of angels are:

A typically benevolent celestial being is an intermediary between Heaven and Earth, especially in Christianity, Judaism, Islam, and Zoroastrianism. They are also seen as a conventional image of a white-robed figure in human form with wings and a halo. People might say that a person regarded as beautiful, good, innocent, and acting like an angel could be an angel. A guiding spirit or influence that helps strengthen humans' spiritual consciousness – may be referred to as a guide.

Where do Angels come from?

Angels, translated in Hebrew, means messenger. Angels are considered the lowest of the nine orders in the Christian celestial hierarchy and appear in Islamic and Judaic traditions. Where do angels stay? Angels are said to dwell in Heaven, but their visits to the earthly realm are not always benevolent. The most famous angel, of course, is Satan, who rebelled against God and was cast out of Heaven. Satan was sent to the deepest depths of a burning hot location with fire and brimstone. Christians call this hell. But what is the real place he was sent to? Could it be a scorching planet or even the sun? Satan visits Earth just like the other benevolent angels, but his work is evil work with us humans. All the benevolent angels stay in Heaven in the furthest depths of the universes. This author believes in our modern terminology that angels come from the many dimensions around our Earth. Angels can easily traverse the dimensions to get to Earth because of all the powers and gifts God has given them. (Merriam-Webster.com)

In reading the Bible, you would find it says that angels are simply people who have died and gone to Heaven. Again, Heaven is not given a location by the Bible except for Heaven. On the other hand, Christians believe that angels are members of a superior race of spiritual beings created before humans. However, some Christians believe angels are not solidly based on the Bible. The Bible, again, says there are quite a few reasons for believing that angels are simply people who have died and come back as angels for being good. Either way, angels being reincarnated humans or superior spiritual beings, they ascend into Heaven (dimensions), as this author's opinion would elude. Science has determined numerous dimensions – like Jesus said, "there are many mansions in Heaven." You also read that I said "reincarnation," many other religions and Bible experts say reincarnation exists. This author believes in reincarnation, that our souls are immortal, and that we pass through dimensions to dwell in another lifeform God creates. (New Church.org)

3

WHAT DO ANGELS LOOK LIKE?

The Bible calls angels "men" or "people." For example, we are told that "the man Gabriel" appeared to Daniel (Daniel 9:21). When angels appeared before all these prophets Abraham (Genesis 18:2), Joshua (Joshua 5:13), Ezekiel (Ezekiel 9:2,3), Zachariah (Zachariah 1:8, 11), and the women of the sepulcher, they called the angels' people. (NewChurch.org) The second reason is that angels look like people. There is no mention in the Bible of angels having wings. The fact that angels appeared before Abraham and Lot said angels did not look different from other people. The people who saw these angels thought they were regular human beings. Paul said, "Do not forget to entertain strangers, for by so doing, some have unwittingly entertained angels" (Hebrews 13:2). The only thing which might distinguish angels from people in appearance is that sometimes the face and clothes of angels appear shining (Daniel 10:6, Matt 28:3, Luke 24:4). It does not mean angels are of a different race; Moses' face also shone after speaking with God (Exodus 34:29), and Jesus said that after death, all good people would "shine forth in the kingdom of their Father" (Matthew 13:43). (New Church.org)

Another reason for believing that angels and men are of the same stock is because they are both described in the same terms. In Hebrew and Greek, the words "angel" mean messenger. These angels are messengers of God. It is one's function or office of an angel, not one's race. It is like the words "King" and "prophet" – it describes the person's function. A messenger could be a human or an angel. Haggai and John the Baptist were called messengers or "angels" of the Lord because they spoke for God (Haggai 1:13, Malachi 3:1). The Bible uses special names to refer to angels, such as "the holy ones." (Daniel 4:13,17), "the sons of God, or even gods (Psalm 30:4), and many other places, usually translated as "saints"), "sons of God" (John 1:12, 1 John 3:1-2). The words that describe angels in the Bible also describe people on Earth. These Biblical accounts of the words used in describing angels also describe people on Earth looking like humans. The Bible never mentions angels being created as a separate race in the creation story: sun, moon, stars, people, animals, fish, and all life. But no angels! (Genesis 1) (newchurch.org) The reason no angels? Because people were created to become angels. Jesus himself said that those worthy become, after death, "equal to angels" (Luke 20:36, Matthew 22:30, Mark 12:25) and would have similar powers.

Understandably, people think angels are superior beings since they have powers and radiance that surpass what we experience on Earth. We can all be transformed into superior beings and become angels after death when we let God live within us. (newchurch.org)

This author thinks angels do not have wings and fly as we were told. The Bible never mentions that angels have wings. They come through Heaven's dimensional veil and are invisible. Angels materialize in human form when they approach their assigned human beings to deliver their messages. Or pass on God's intentions for that person. The Bible does describe angels as looking like people but having a glow to them. Moses had a bright glow to him after he spoke to God. Not mentioned was how long Moses glowed brightly. Moses was filled with the divine spirit.

Angels are personal spirit beings created to worship and serve God. We don't know when angels were created concerning the events of Genesis (1-2). Scripture indicates angels were present when God created the Earth (Job 38;4-7). There seems to be a little confusion about when angels were created and if they were humans before being an angel. Angels are mysterious to us, powerful beings, but God created them like all things. Angels are part of the "invisible" things and "power" that God created and mentioned by Paul: "In [the Son] all things were created: things in Heaven and on Earth, visible and invisible, all things have been created for him and through him. God is before all things" (Colossians 1:16-17) (GotQuestions.org)

We know how God made man here on Earth. God scooped up some mud, formed Adam's body, then breathed life into it, and man became a living soul (Genesis 2:7). We are not told how God made angels or what "substance," if any, God used. Did he breathe or speak the angels into existence? Angels could be part of God's thoughts that brought angels into existence. It is just another aspect of God's creative brilliance.

Does this sound like another theory or interpretation of what angels are? The popular notion I spoke about earlier is that people become angels when they die – at least, the good people do. There is no Biblical basis for this theory that angels are former people. Confusing? Yes! In one interpretation, angels are different from us humans; mankind is a class of being created "a little lower than the angels" (Psalm 8:5). Even in Heaven, the difference between humanity and the "angel kind" is differentiated (Revelation 7:9-11). (GotQuestions.org)

This author's confusion comes from people claiming that friendly and good people are angels. Whatever the Biblical interpretation, I believe good people go to Heaven and are angels when they get there. I think God first created angels through His brilliance with spiritual energy when he created the Earth and the universe. Angels don't have wings, but that doesn't say they can't create wings for the human eyes to behold. Angels are invisible, and God gave them powers to accomplish their missions here on Earth. Angels' wings are symbolic of the ability to fly. They need no wings to move around through dimensions and to humans on Earth on their missions for God. Angels can traverse time and space. Angels act under direction from God rather than their own volition and expect nothing in return.

4

GOD DIRECTS ANGELS TO GUARD AND PROTECT US

God sends his angels to deliver messages to us using words like "Do not be afraid" or "Do not Fear." God's angels operate discretely and don't draw attention to themselves as they carry out assignments God gave them. While God has called His heavenly messengers to work on His behalf, He also called angels to work in our lives in profound ways. There are many stories of people saying angels have performed miracles for them. Without their guardian angel, they would not be alive. Angels are to protect us and fight for us if need be. That means they are working on our behalf. (Beliefnet)

The Bible tells us, "For He will command His angels concerning you to guard you in all your ways. On their hands, they will bear you up, lest you strike your foot against a stone" (Psalm 91:11-12). God sent His angel for Daniel's protection, and he shut the lion's mouth. God offers His pure and selfless love using His angels. Throughout the Bible, we find angels involved in communicating God's truth or message as the spirit of God directed them. In the Bible, in several passages, we are told that angels were instruments used by God to reveal his word. (Leslie White) (Beliefnet)

Angels revealing God's word is only part of the story. There are several times when angels appear to announce an important message. While there are other times angels have sent words of comfort and reassurance, they also deliver messages of warnings, telling of judgments, and even carrying out assessments. The Bible tells us, "For we are made a spectacle unto the world and the angels and men" (1 Corinthians 4:9). According to scripture, there are many eyes upon us, including the eyes of angels. We are being watched according to God's will. A spectacle means "theater" or "public assembly." Angels gain knowledge from us by watching over us and our activities intently. Humans study the past, but angels do not have to study history; they have experienced it. With past knowledge, angels can predict how humans may act in similar circumstances.

God sends angels to encourage us and guide us on the path we need to take. In Acts, angels encourage early followers of Jesus to begin their ministry, free Paul and others from prison, and facilitate meetings with believers and non-believers. Angels have great strength through God's powers. The apostle Paul calls them "mighty angels" (2 Thessalonians 1:17). The power of a single angel was demonstrated in part of the resurrection morning (Matthew 28:2). While angels can excel in strength, we must remember that God is omnipotent. Another way angels work for us is through deliverance. Angels are always involved in the lives of God's people. They have specific functions, and it is a blessing that God sends them to respond to our specific9 times of need. (Beliefnet)

The Bible tells us, "Are not all angels ministering spirits sent to serve those who will inherit salvation?" (Hebrews 1:14). Because of this specific role in our lives, they can visit us and warn and protect us from harm. Nobody knows when that will happen in the end times – there has been speculation on that day, but only God and His angels know. There will come a time when we move into our Heavenly homes and be assisted by angels. The angels will be with us when leaving our physical bodies. The primary scripture teachings of Christ told us of the angels helping us in Heaven. In Luke 16, in describing the beggar Lazarus' death, Jesus said, "So it was that the beggar died, and was carried by angels to Abraham's bosom," referring to Heaven. Lazarus wasn't merely escorted to Heaven. The angels carried him there. This is all possible what angels do for us, humans. It is that God commissions angels to care for His children. Angels are invisible to us most of the time, but our lives are surrounded by angels here to assist us in our times of need, including death. (Beliefnet)

5

SPIRIT GUIDES

There are six types of spirit guides. You have spirit guides sending you helpful messages no matter who you are, what you look like, or where you come from. I will help you find out who your unique guides are with the following information. Open your consciousness for their wisdom and communicate with your guides through prayer and meditation. Spirit guides stay with you for your entire life. God gave us free will to request more spirit guides to help us. Your team of guides assigned to you could include any of the six guides.

Archangels

Archangels are the leaders in the angel world and have a powerful, very large energy signature. If you are an empath or sensitive to energy, when you call on an Archangel, you might feel the energy shift in the room. Each archangel has a particular function, like Archangel Raphael's healing specialty. Raphael can work on countless humans at once. (www.mindbodygreen.com)

Guardian Angels

Guardian Angels are exclusively your angel, and we have more than one angel to protect us. Guardian angels are devoted to helping you only. You can call on these angels at any time for fast assistance. These Guardian angels will love you unconditionally, forever. Angels are nondenominational and work with people of all faiths and beliefs.

Spirit Animals

Spirit animals could be pets you once owned or knew from other peoples' pets. Your pet could have passed away and now is part of your spiritual guidance squad. The animal spirit guide could be any animal with something to teach you, like a peacock teaching you how to be beautiful or a wolf teaching you survival lessons. Spirit animals can show up in dreams and help you answer your problem, or animals in your backyard can also show you a message. (www.mind-bodygreen.com)

Ascended Masters

Ascended Masters like Buddha or Mother Mary were once human, living journeys of profound spiritual growth. They hold unique places as leaders in the spirit world and as guides/teachers to humans. These Ascended Masters are partners and work together in harmony, regardless of culture or religion.

Departed Loved Ones

Loved ones you knew and members of your family who have passed away may choose to be one of your spirit guides and actively support you from Heaven. They help in practical ways, like sending career opportunities or loving relationships your way. A past grandmother could be an essential spirit guide whether you knew her. Any human who passed away could be your spirit guide, even if you did not know them well. A musician or dancer who passed away could be your spirit guide and inspire you as an artist. (www.mindbodygreen.com)

Helper Angels

These angels are not committed to one person but travel to any human who needs extra help. Helper angels help find friends or a new home.

How do Spirit Guides Communicate with Humans?

Spirit guides will send us signs when they enter our lives, also called synchronicities. Carl Jung defined synchronicities as "a meaningful coincidence." An example is when you disagree with your spouse about communications; you see a book about marital communications the next day on someone's desk. This next synchronicity is very popular. This is when your spirit guides communicate to you with number sequences like 111, 11, 33, 3,6, and 9 numbers. Or you might have a lucky number, and when you see someone about a job, their address has your lucky number. Musical messages are also something your spirit guides would communicate with you, like when you get in your car, and the radio is playing the song you just heard in your head. It could also be a song you and your favorite person enjoy hearing together. Spirit guides can be in your dreams, showing you how to handle a particular problem, or a guide could appear in your dreams. (www.mindbodygreen.com)

Your spirit guides could use a combination of signs besides numbers. The dreams spirit guides send you while you could be a rehearsal for what is to come the next day or next month. I have had many dreams that foretold future events that I will witness. My dreams included plant closure, a very ill friend, and a journey to another dimension. Can spirit guides show you the future? Yes. People have told me that their dreams come true and are very lucid. If any outside influence on our dreams can happen, our spirit guides would plant a seed for what is to come.

I have to say that synchronicity numbers are the most popular with people. Everybody sees the numbers 11 and 33 and takes a special mental note of the observation. What are the spirit guides telling us? We are still trying to find the significance of 3,6 and 9, which people like Nikola Tesla and Albert Einstein say are the universe's secret numbers. Maybe the spirit guides give us clues to break the total consciousness and spiritual power code. When I get an important call, or someone needs me, I will see the numbers 11 and 33. Imagination or spirit guide tells me that this is synchronicity and an essential issue in your life.

6

ARE ANGELS MALE OR FEMALE? WHAT ARE THE BIBLE FACTS?

As the Bible states, angels are not male or female in how humans understand and experience gender. Most references in the Bible describe angels as men. According to Christian theology, angels are wholly spiritual beings and therefore do not eat, excrete or have sex, and have no gender. This brings up a thought in this author's mind: Isn't Mother Mary an angel? To interject an opinion here, I would like to state that I have seen angelic women in white hooded gowns that appeared to be angels. Other people have seen women like angels in gowns. We will get to that soon in this book.

Due to the association with beauty, Jophiel is one of the few angels sometimes portrayed as female. Angels have no canonical gender and are commonly referred to as male pronouns. We must ask ourselves, can a girl be an angel? In this author's opinion, I would have to say yes. Most references to angels in the Bible and religious texts describe them as men, but sometimes they're women. Confusing, right? People that have seen angels describe them as being both male and female. Witnesses to angels report them as being of both sexes. The same angel (such as Archangel Gabriel) shows up sometimes as a man and other times as a woman. (www.learnreligions.com)

Who was the first female angel?

Many feminists see Lilith as not only the first independent woman created. In the creation story, she refuses to allow Adam to dominate her and flees the garden despite the consequences. She had to give up her children, and in retaliation, she steels the seed of Adam.

Lilith is a female figure in Mesopotamian and Judaic mythology, alternately the first wife of Adam and primordial she-demon. Lilith was "banished" from the Garden of Eden for not complying and obeying Adam. Lilith is mentioned in Biblical Hebrew in the Book of Isaiah and late Antiquity in Mandaean mythology and Jewish mythology sources from 500 CE onward. The Book of Adam and Eve mentions her in the Babylonian Talmud (Eruvin 100b, Niddah 24b, Shabbat 151b, Baba Bathra 73a). She is mentioned in the Book of Adam and Eve as Adam's wife and "a hot fiery female who first cohabitated with man." Lilith stems from Lilu and (and (w)ardat Lili). The Hebrew word Lilith in (Isaiah 34:14) is thought to be a night bird by some modern scholars such as Judith M. Blair. In Sumer, Assyria, and Babylonia, Lilith signifies a spirit or demon.

The Biblical Lilith inspired authors like the first Jewish feminist theologian Judith Plaskow to write "The Coming of Lilith," examining patriarchal dominance in Judaism and Christianity, and writing "Which Lilith?" Lilith continues as a source of popular culture, Western culture, and Literature. Lilith is also mentioned in Occultism, fantasy, and horror with the events of men experiencing the old hag syndrome with a woman on their chest while they sleep, making it hard to breathe. I never had that experience, but I know Guys who have had the old hag syndrome. The Biblical interpretation says that Lilith is a demon angel, making her presence felt by men. She is often depicted as a woman fighting for equality and striving for fairness. (Wikipedia.org)

Lilith is stated in the Dictionary of Deities and Demons in the Bible (1999); Lilith appears in a Mandaean magic story where she is considered to represent the branches of a tree with other demonic figures that form the different parts of the tree. However, it might show other multiple Liliths. The connection between Gilgamesh and the Jewish Lilith was rejected by Sergio Ribichini (1978). The Bible mentions Lilith only once, as a dweller in waste places (Isaiah 34:14). Lilith was considered the seducer or slayer of children and had a long prehistory in ancient Babylonian religion. Lilith is responsible for males' erotic dreams and night emissions. Just as mentioned earlier about the old hag syndrome. (Wikipedia)

The demon is also spelled daemon. Angels and demons, respectively, are any benevolent or malevolent spiritual beings that mediate between the transcendent and temporal realms. Throughout the history of religions, various beliefs have existed in various spiritual beings, powers, and principles that mediate between the realm of the sacred or holy: the transcendent realm—and the profane realm of time, space, and cause and effect. Angels in Judaism, Christianity, and

Islam, and those viewed as malevolent, are called demons. Intermediate beings are less categorical, for they may be benevolent in some cases and malevolent in others. These spiritual beings can be confused about their mission for humans. Thus, angels have their significance primarily in what they do rather than what they are; whatever essence or inherent nature they possess is their relationship to their source (God or the ultimate being). Lilith was the first demon angel, not a good spiritual angel as most angels are in the Bible. Of course, we have the fallen angels that were cast out of Heaven that were made up mostly of male angels who turned against God. These fallen angels make up the evil bad demonic angels that fight against good and God. (Wikipedia)

The First Female Named Angel – Jophiel

The angel Jophiel (Heb, Yopiel), "God is my beauty [alternatively: Beauty of God"], "divine beauty"), also called Iophiel, Jofiel, Youfiel, Zophiel, "spy of God," "watchman of God"), and Zuriel, "my rock is God," is a non-canonical archangel of wisdom, understanding, and judgment. She is listed as one of the seven Archangels in pseudo-Dionysian teachings. Due to her association with beauty, Jophiel is one of the few angels to be sometimes portrayed as female. However, angels do not have a canonical gender, and male pronouns refer to most. According to the Revelation of Moses, another name for Jophiel is Dina. Jophiel is described as an angel of the seventh Heaven, a Cabalistic guardian of the Torah and wisdom itself; she taught seventy languages to souls at the dawn of creation. The Zohar list Jophiel as a Great Angel Chief in charge of fifty-three legions who oversaw Torah readings on the Sabbath. In her book Angels in Art, C.E. Clement names Jophiel as a teacher of Ham, Japheth, and Shem.

In Anglican and Episcopal traditions, Jophiel is recognized as an archangel. She is often depicted in iconography holding a flaming sword, such as the stained glasses at St. Michael's Church in Brighton and St. Peter's and St. John's Church in Kirkley, U.K. In the U.S., you can see a mural at St. John's Episcopal Church in Memphis, Tennessee, with Jophiel holding a flaming sword. Jophiel, according to Arthur de Bles, and R.L. Giles, Jophiel was said to be the Angel who cast Adam and Eve out of Paradise. Jophiel oversees the Cherubim, particularly the angels Haziel, Aladiah, Lauviah, Iezalel, Mehahel, Hariel, and Hakamiah.

Angels of Love and Light describes Jophiel as "the Archangel of Paradise and the Patron of Artists and Illumination." She teaches the outer consciousness the power of light within oneself. She stirs feelings through Radiation and Illumination and into aspiration for spiritual things. Jophiel helps absorb information, study for and pass tests, dissolve ignorance, pride, and narrow-mindedness, and expose government wrongdoing.

After talking about Jophiel (woman angel) on this book's last page, we get into the Bible scriptures that talk about the masculine gender, only referring to angels. A feminine form of Angelos does not exist. There are three genders in grammar – masculine (he, him, his), feminine (she, her, hers), and neuter (it, its). Angels are never referred to other than males in the scriptures. When angels appear to people, they are always dressed as males (Genesis 18:2, 16: Ezekiel 9:2). I have a question about female angels I will discuss later. The devil, whom we assume is a fallen angel, is also referred to in masculine terms: he is a "father" in John 8:44.

People point to Zechariah 5:9 as an example of female angels. That verse says, "Then I looked up and there before I was two women, with the wind in their wings! The problem is that the "women" in this prophetic vision are not called angels. They are called Nashim (women), as is the woman in the basket representing wickedness in verses 7 and 8. Zechariah spoke to the angel called a Malak, a completely different word meaning "angel" or "messenger." A vision does not necessarily depict actual beings or objects – consider the huge flying scroll Zechariah sees earlier in the same chapter (Zechariah 5:1-2). In Matthew 22:30, Jesus says there will be no marriage in Heaven because we "will be like the angels in Heaven." The verse states that angels do not marry because there are no genders in Heaven. God is spirit (John 4:4) and does not have a "gender" any more than angels do with the neuter noun pneuma ("spirit"). (Wikipedia)

Some Confusions About Angels

In (NASB) Bible Genesis 6:1-2, when men began to multiply on the face of the land, and daughters were born of them. The sons of God saw the daughters of men were beautiful, and they took wives for themselves, whomever they chose.

The phrase "son of God" refers to angels (Job 1:6; 2:1). There is also a reference in Jude to this event in Genesis, but there is no statement that the angels had gender.

These angels did not keep their domain but abandoned their proper abode. God has kept in eternal bonds under darkness for the judgment of the great day, just as Sodom and Gomorrah and the cities around them. Since they, in the same way as these, indulged in gross immorality and went after strange flesh, they are exhibited as an example of undergoing the punishment of eternal fire. (NASB Jude 1:6-7). The phrase "indulged in gross immorality" does not say they had a gender. We don't know how they possessed the women. The passage does not say they "knew" the women. A typical expression in scripture is "knew" for a man and woman having sex. These angels sinned and were cast into an abyss as their punishment. God's angels are His ministers who do his bidding. Those who do not are punished. Sadly, almost every painting, photograph, sculpture, and image of angels' presents angels as females. Such angels, if they existed, would be evil angels. The Bible never states that female angels exist or that angels have gender. They are always referred to as males. God's master design, the male, has the leadership in the home, society, and the church. (What does the Bible say? Never thirsty)

Sons of God

Some believe another passage in the Bible indicates that angels have gender. Genesis 6:1-2 tells us that the "sons of God" took wives from among women.

7

ANGELS INTERPRETED BY OTHER RELIGIONS

Zoroastrianism

There was a belief in the Amesha Spentas, the holy or bounteous immortals, who were functional aspects or entities of Ahura Mazda, the Wise Lord. The Amesha Spentas, Vohu Manah (Good Mind), revealed to the Iranian prophet Zarathustra (Zoroaster; died c. 551 BCE) the true God, his nature, and his kind of ethical covenant, which humans may accept and obey or reject and disobey. About 1,200 years later, archangel Gabriel revealed to the Prophet Muhammad (5th-6th century CE) the Qur'an (the holy book of Islam) and the true God (Allah), his oneness, and the ethical and cultic requirements of Islam. The epithets used to describe Gabriel, the messenger of God – "the spirit of holiness" and the faithful spirit" – are similar to those applied to the Amesha Spentas of Zoroastrianism and the holy spirit, the third person of the trinity (Father, Son, and Holy Spirit), in Christianity. We will get more into the Islamic religion later in this book. (Britannia Angels& Demons)

In these monotheistic religions (through Zoroastrianism later became dualistic) as in Judaism, the functional characteristics of angels are more clearly enunciated than their ontological (or nature of being) characteristics – except in instances in which popular piety and legend have glossed over the functional aspects. Various religions, including those of nonliterate cultures, have beliefs in intermediary beings between the sacred and profane realms, but the idea is most fully elaborate in religions of the west. In these descriptions, you can see where other faiths felt there were intermediaries, like angels being messengers of God. Or were these angel beliefs and concepts passed down through other religions thousands of years previously taught?

In Zoroastrianism, there are different angel-like figures. Each person has a guardian angel called Fravashi. They patronize human beings and other creatures and manifest God's energy. As we spoke about Amesha Spentas, they have often been called angels, although there is no direct reference to them conveying messages rather than emanations of Ahura Mazda (Wise Lord, God); they later appeared abstractly and then later became personalized, associated with various aspects of creation. (Wikipedia.org)

Etymology

The word angel arrives in modern English from the old English Engel (with a hard g) and the Old French angele. Both words came from the Late Latin angelus, which in turn was borrowed from the Greek angelos (literally "messenger"). Angelos might be "an Oriental loan, like (angaros, Persian mounted courier)." The word "angelos" is the default translation of the Biblical Hebrew term malakh, denoting simply "messenger" without connoting its nature. In the Latin Vulgate, this meaning becomes bifurcated: words like nuntius or legatus are applied that indicate human messenger. When referring to angels as supernatural beings, the word angelus appears. Such differentiation has been taken over by later vernacular translations of the Bible, early Christians, Jewish exegetes, and modern scholars.

Judaism

In Judaism, angels (Hebrew: Malak: "messenger") are understood through interpretations of the Tanakh and in long tradition as supernatural beings who stand by God in Heaven but are strictly distinguished from God (YHWH) and are subordinate to HIM. These angels can show selected people God's will and instructions. In a different twist, in the Jewish tradition, they are considered inferior to humans since angels have no will. Angels have no free will and can only carry out one divine command for God.

Hebrew Bible

The Torah uses the Hebrew Bible with terms like (Malak Elohim: messenger of God"), (Malak Yahweh; "messenger of the Lord), (bane Elohim; "sons of God"), and (haqqodasim; the holy ones") referring to beings traditionally interpreted as angels. Later texts used other terms such as (ha elyonim; "the upper ones"). The term (Malak) is also used in other books of the Hebrew Bible. The Hebrew word may refer to a human messenger or a supernatural messenger. A prophet or priest could have been a human messenger, such as Malachi, "my messenger"; the Greek superscription translation states the Book of Malachi was written, "by the hand of his messenger" (angelu). Examples of a supernatural messenger are the Malak YHWH," who is either a messenger of God, an aspect of God, or God Himself as the messenger (the theophanic angel.") (Wikipedia.org)

Quoting Michael D. Coogan, only in the later books that the terms "come to mean the benevolent semi-divine beings familiar from later mythology and art." The book of Daniel, the biblical book, refers to individual angels by name, mentioning Gabriel in Daniel 9:21 and Michael in Daniel 10:13. These two angels are part of Daniel's apocalyptic visions and are part of the apocalyptic literature.

In Daniel 7, Daniel receives a dream vision from God. As Daniel watches his dream vision from God, the ancient of Days takes his seat on the throne of Heaven and sits in judgment amid a Heavenly court, an {angel} like a son of man approaches the Ancient One in the clouds of Heaven and is given everlasting kingship. The development of this concept of angels: "In the postexilic period, with the development of monotheism, these divine beings- the "sons of God" who were members of the Divine Council-were in effect demoted to what are known as "angels," they were created by God, but immortal and thus superior to humans. My thoughts are that we are told we are all immortal, with our soul/spirit returning to God. This conception of angels contrasts with demons and is often thought to be "influenced by the ancient Persian religious tradition of Zoroastrianism, which viewed the world as a battleground between forces of good and evil. (Michael D. Coogan)

Abrahamic Religions

Abrahamic religion often depicts angels as benevolent celestial intermediaries between God (or Heaven) and humanity. This religion also includes angels being protectors and guides for humans and servants of God. Abrahamic religion describes angelic hierarchies, which vary in religion and sect. Some angels have specific names (such as Gabriel or Michael) or titles (such as seraph or archangel). Those expelled from Heaven are the fallen angels, distinct from the Heavenly host. They include Satan, who parted ways with God, bringing about the fight between good and evil and light and darkness. One of these is Hassatan, a figure depicted in (among other places) the Book of Job.

Later interpretations, according to Kabbalah, there are four worlds, and our world is the last: the world of action (Assiyah). Angels exist in the worlds above as a task of God. Angels are extensions of God to produce effects in this world. After the angels complete their job, it ceases to exist. The angel, in effect, is the task that God gives them to perform. This information is derived from the book of Genesis when Abraham meets with three angels, and Lot meets with two angels.

The task of the angels for Abraham was to inform Sara and Abraham of their coming child. Angels that visited Lot were to save Lot and his family from the destruction of Sodom and Gomorrah. (Wikipedia)

Rabbinic Judaism

According to Rabbinic Judaism, the angels have no bodies but are eternally living creatures created out of fire and occasionally appear in Midrashim as competition with humans. As you can see from these statements, the Rabbinic religion believes angels are eternal, whereas other religions say angels cease to exist when they complete their tasks. Heavenly beings strictly follow the laws of God and become jealous of God's affection for man. This last statement is different than other interpretations by saying angels get jealous of God and man's relationship. Angels are said to be wholly spiritual and can't be jealous of man because they serve man through God's laws. Humans, by following the Torah, in prayer, resisting evil instincts (yetzer hara), and by Teshuva, are preferred to the flawless angels. As a result, they are also inferior to humans in the Jewish tradition. The Midrash, the plural of El (Elohim) used in Genesis about the creation of humans, is explained by the presence of angels: God consulted with the angels but left the final decision to God. This story is an example that the powerful should consult with the weak. This statement guides humans to listen to others and give equal opinions on decisions.

Certain angels took on particular significance and developed unique personalities and roles. If angels took on different personalities, it was mostly to match the human emotions; they are helping. Archangels were believed to rank among the Heavenly host; no systematic hierarchy ever developed. Metatron is considered one of the highest angels in Merkabah and Kabbalah mysticism. Metatron often serves as a scribe; he is briefly mentioned in Talmud and figures prominently in Merkabah's mystical text. Were these angels considered mystical, as stated in this past remark? As we enter each religion, we see different beliefs and approaches to angels. Archangel Michael was always considered a warrior and fought for Israel (Daniel 10:13) is looked upon particularly fondly by most religions. Gabriel, another very popular angel in most beliefs, is mentioned in the book of Daniel (Daniel 8:15-17) and briefly in the Talmud. The Judaism religion did not worship angels, and there is no evidence for the invocation and conjuration of angels.

Philo of Alexandria identifies angels as the immaterial voice of God. He claims angels are different from God but conceived as God's instruments.

There are four classes of ministering angels minister and utter praises to God the Holy One, blessed be He: first camp (led by) Michael on God's right, second camp (directed by) Gabriel on God's left, third camp (led by) Uriel before God, and the fourth camp (led by) Raphael behind God; and the Shekhinah of the Holy One, blessed be God, is in the center. (Wikipedia.org)

Buddhism Angels

The Buddhist equivalent of angels is devas or celestial beings. Some schools of Buddhism refer to dharma palas or dharma protectors. The Tibetan Buddhism, devas are emanations of bodhisattvas or enlightened beings. Various schools of Buddhism have important devas, often derived from pre-Buddhist cultures and religions and not from Buddhist philosophy.

Divas are spiritual beings by nature-their form and are usually described as bodies or emanations of light energy. Often depicted in physical form, there are many images of devas or dharma palas, mainly in Tibetan Buddhist iconography. Most of the time, Devas do not interfere in human affairs, but the Buddhist teacher Lama Surya Das notes that they have been known to rejoice, applaud, and rain down flowers for good deeds in the world.

The Thailand Buddhists believe that devas approve of people meditating and will harass people whose behavior they don't approve of. The bodhisattva of compassion, known as Kwan Yin in Chinese and Chenrezig in Tibetan, is widely regarded as a Buddhist angel. The bodhisattva's original Sanskrit name, Avolokiteshvara, means "hearer of the 10,000 cries" – that is, he or she (the bodhisattva is a male in the original Buddhist texts but is represented as a female in many Buddhist schools) perceives the suffering of all sentient beings. In some sects, reciting her name is believed to summon her aid.

Hinduism Angels

Hinduism does not explicitly refer to spiritual beings as angels; however, Hinduism *does* have many different types of spirit beings who act in a similar capacity. An example is the minor gods, or devas, literally "shining ones," who inhabit the higher astral plane. Gods, devas, planets like Sani (Saturn), gurus (teachers), and ancestors can all play protective roles for humans. Also, part of Hinduism are asuras, evil spirits, and demons. There are fallen devas like in the old testament's Christian belief of fallen angels. These fallen divas inhabit the lower astral plane, the mental plane of existence. If the asuras do good on Earth, they can be reincarnated into devas and do not have to stay in the lower plane. Hinduism also includes apsaras, Heavenly nymphs, angiris, who preside over sacrifices, and lipika, who regulate karma. The devas and apsaras are spiritual beings like angels. But they are often depicted in physical form. The apsaras are seductively beautiful, and the devas often look like royalty, stately and handsome. These two devas and asuras can inspire or bring down aspirants; they can help or hinder people's spiritual journey. (guideangel.com)

There are six, possibly seven, human body energy centers called chakras, and how they are connected to the kabbalistic and Christian angelic systems. According to traditional Hinduism medicine, Chakra refers to wheel-like vortices believed to exist on the body's surface.

These chakras are force centers or whorls of energy permeating the whole body. The layers of subtle bodies are in an ever-increasing fan-shaped formation (the fans make the shape of a love heart). These seven chakra centers are considered the focal points for the reception and transmission of spiritual energies. Seven major Chakra centers or energy centers, also called wheels of light (angels), are generally believed to exist within the subtle body.

Practitioners of Hinduism believe the chakras interact with the body's ductless endocrine glands and lymphatic system by feeding on good bio-energies and disposing of unwanted bio-energies. Most information on Chakras comes from the Upanishads, which are difficult to date. The information about Chakras is difficult to date because they are believed to have been passed down orally at least a thousand years before being written down. The earliest writings are between 1200-900 BCE. (guideangel.com/angels)

The Hinduism concept of chakras is part of a complex of ideas related to esoteric anatomy. These ideas often occur in the class of texts called Agamas or Tantras. These are a large body of scriptures. There are many variations on these concepts in the Sanskrit source texts. In earlier texts, various systems of chakras and nadis have varying connections. Traditional sources list 5,6,7 or 8 chakras. Over time one scenario of 6 or 7 chakras along the body's axis became the dominant model. Most schools of yoga adopted this concept. The latter system, with one less chakra point, originated in about the 11th century AD and became widely popular. In this model, Kundalini is said to "rise" upward, piercing the various centers until reaching the crown of the head, resulting in union with the divine.

Chakra locations:

Root (Muladhara), last bone in the spinal cord – Communicate with Angels – Foundation/wholly remembering/ coherent knowledge

Sacrum (Swadhisthana) sacrum – human prostate/ovaries – communicate with "Principalities"- Contemplation/Initiative/persistence

Solar Plexus (Manipura) (navel area) of humans – Communicate with the "Archangels" – Surrender/sincerity/steadfastness

Heart (Anahata) middle of the chest – heart location of human – Symmetry/balance/compassion

Throat (Vishuddha), middle of the throat on humans – communicates with "Dominions" – Mercy/Grace/Love of (intention to emulate) God and for communicating with the "Virtues" – Judgement/strength/determination.

Third Eye (Ajna) Brow of the forehead on humans – (pineal gland or third eye) serves as communication with Cherubim from Chokmah – the Divine Reality/revelation – Understanding/repentance/reason.

The Crown of the head (Sahasrara) on top of the head of the human – a soft spot of the newborn – serves to communicate with the "Seraphim" – Crown Divine Plan/Creator (guideangel.com/angels)

Angels in the Islam

Belief in angels is one of the six pillars of Islamic belief, without which there is no faith. In Islam, if you don't believe in angels, you are declared to not be a believer (mu'min). The pillars are a belief in Allah, His Books, His Messengers, the Last Day, and that good and bad predestination comes from Allah. Angels are a part of the world of the Unseen which we cannot comprehend. Allah spoke about angels in many places in the Qur'an via His Prophet Muhammad. There have been proven reports concerning the angels that will make you realize the Creator's greatness and this religion's greatness.

Of what are they created?

Muslim religion says angels are made of light, as Aa'ishah reported. Allah's Messenger said: "The angels are created from light, just as the jinn are created from smokeless fire. Mankind is created from what you have been told about." (Reported by Muslim, no. 2996). They have wings. Allah says (interpretation of the meaning): "Praise be to Allah, who created (out of nothing) the Heavens and the Earth, Who made the angels messengers with wings – two, or three, or four (pairs) adds to creation as He pleases: for Allah has power over all things." [Faatir 35:1]

Angels differ in size and status; there are differences between them, just as in virtues. The best of the angels are those present at the battle of Badr, as stated in the hadeeth narrated by Mu aadh ibn Rifaa'ah al-Zuraaqi from his father, who was present at Badr. He said: "Jibreel came to the Prophet and asked, how do you rate the people among you who were present at Badr?" He said: "They are the best of the Muslims, or something similar. Jibreel said: "So it is with the angels who were present at Badr." (Reported by al-Bukhaari, no. 3992).

Muslims also believe angels do not eat or drink. This finding came from a conversation between Ibraaheem, the "friend" of Allaah, and the angels who visited him. Then Allaah told his household to bring out the fatted calf, and they placed it before the angels. He said, "will you not eat?" (When they did not want to eat), he became filled with fear of the angels. Angels said, "fear not," and they gave him tidings of a son endowed with knowledge." [al-Dhaariyaat 51:26-28]

There are many angels, and their number is known only to Allah, this is called their angel number. The Prophet said, described the Much-Frequented House (al-Bayt al-Ma'moor) in the seventh Heaven: "Then I was taken up to the Much-Frequented House: every day seventy thousand angels visit it and leave, never returning to it again, another [group] coming after them. (Reported by al-Bukhaari, Fath, no. 3207). Prior to Islam, angels were daughters of God and worshipped in pre-Islamic Arabia. But the notion that God created the angels as females and fathered daughters is rejected in the Quran. Angels have names; just like all other religions, Muslims have names for angels. (guideangel.com)

But we know only a few names of angels. We must believe in the names reported in the Qur'an and Sunnah texts, as a general belief in the angels. Among the names of angels that are known to us are: In Islam, four angels are well known: Jibril (Gabriel), the angel of revelation; Mikal (Michael), the angel of nature; Izrail (Azrael), the angel of death, and Israfil, the angel who places the soul in the body and sounds the last judgment. This and all angel information in this book is summarized. More about the angels in Islam is on this page: Al-Malaa'ikah (Angels) from Islam. (guideangel.com)

Summarizing the Various Religions and Angel Beliefs

In my research, I have found that different religions have varying viewpoints about angels in regard to their faith. Islam belief has four angels they believe in that are important to their Quran and Allaah. In Hinduism, they have many spiritual beings that they say are numerous, and they call them devas or small gods. They are spiritual entities that live on a higher plane. Hinduism is a diversified religion on many levels. From Divas to the six or seven Chakra energy locations on the human body. Buddhism is like Hinduism, whereas they call angels divas spiritual beings. Judaism is like the Christian belief in that it believes in angels from the Bible verses of Genesis. All religions covered in this book will list the differences they share with other beliefs. This is just a sampling of the material discussed in this book.

Angels in Christianity Summary

Christianity embraced angels like no religion before or even after Christianity started. Throughout the Bible, it is implied that each soul has its tutelary angel. Abraham, when sending his steward to seek a wife for Issac, says, "He will send his angel before thee" (Genesis 24:7). The nineteenth Psalm, which the devil quoted to our Lord (Matt., iv,6) is well known, and Judith accounts for her heroic deed by saying: "As the Lord liveth, His angel hath been my keeper" (xiii, 20).

These passages and many like them (Gen., xvi, 6-32: Osec, xii, 4; Ps., xxxiii, 8) will not themselves demonstrate the doctrine that every individual has his appointed guardian angel and receive their compliment in our Savior's words: "See that you despise not one of these little ones; for I say to you that their angels in Heaven always see the face of My Father Who is in Heaven" (Matt, xviii, 10), words which illustrate the remark of St. Augustine: "What lies hidden in the Old Testament, is made manifest in the New." Our Lord says: "The dignity of a soul is so great that each has a guardian angel from its birth." (guideangel.com)

In Christianity, angels were highly revered by all who believed, and angels are one of the main pillars of the Christian foundation. God depended on angels to care for humans as his messengers in Christianity.

8

WATCHERS

Watcher (Aramaic, plural 'iyrin; Theodotian trans: from the root of Hebrew," awake, watchful." "Watchers," "those who are awake,"; "guard," "watcher," "a type of Biblical angel. Watcher occurs in the plural and singular forms in the Book of Daniel (fourth-second century BC), where references are made to their holiness. The Apocryphal Books of Enoch (second-first centuries BC) refer to both good and bad Watchers, focusing on the rebellious ones.

The Book of Daniel

In the Book of Daniel 4:13, 17, 23 (ESV), three references to the class of "watcher, holy one" (Holy One, Aramaic qaddiysh). The term is introduced by Nebuchadnezzar, who says he saw "a watcher, a holy one come down (singular verb) from Heaven. "The watcher told Nebuchadnezzar to eat grass and be mad and that this was his punishment." The watcher told him that this is "by the decree of the watchers, the demand by the word of the holy ones" ...." the living may know that the Most High rules in the kingdom of men." Throughout Biblical history, Prophets and Kings were communicated to by God with dreams and visions. In our modern times, we have seemed to forget this human talent of listening to God. Ancient Biblical text says: "be still and listen for God's instructions." When humans have dreams and visions now, they don't know how to connect the actual message from God. We will talk later about visions. (Wikipedia.org)

King Nebuchadnezzar envisioned another dream that a watcher that came down from Heaven saying, "Chop down the tree and destroy it but leave the stump of its roots in the earth, bound with a band of iron and bronze, in the tender grass of the field, till seven periods of time pass over him and let his portion be with the beasts of the field. This is the interpretation, O King: It is a decree of the Most High, which has come upon my Lord the King, that you shall be driven from among men, and your dwelling shall be with the beasts of the field. You will be made to eat grass like an ox, and you shall be wet with the dew of Heaven. Seven periods shall pass over you till you know (understand) the Most High rules the kingdom of men and gives it to whom he will. This is saying that God will choose your place in man's kingdom, not a King. This did not come to fruition throughout history because Kings still ruled over men and chose their destinies.

Protestant reformer Johann Wigand better explains it viewed the watcher in Nebuchadnezzar's dream as either God himself or the Son of God. Johann promoted Trinitarian thinking by linking verse 17 ("This matter is by the decree of the watchers") with verse 24 ("this is the decree of the Most High"). Most Scholars view "watchers, holy ones" as perhaps showing an influence of Babylonian gods recognizing the power of the god of Israel as "Most High." The Greek Septuagint version differs from the Aramaic Text: for example, the Aramaic Text is ambiguous about who is telling the story of verse 14, whether it is the King or the watcher in his dream. (Wikipedia.org/wiki/Watcher)

Books of Enoch and watchers

The term "watchers" is common in the Book of Enoch. The Book of the Watchers (1 Enoch 6-36) occurs in the Aramaic fragments with the phrase irin we-qadis hin, "Watchers and Holy Ones," a reference to Aramaic Daniel. The Aramaic irin "watcher" is rendered as "angel" (Greek angelos, Coptic malah). The usual Aramaic term for angel malakha does not occur in Aramaic Enoch. The First Book of Enoch devotes much of its attention to the watchers' fall. Enoch's second book addresses the watchers (Gk. Egre goroi) in the fifth Heaven where the fall occurred. Enock's third Book gives attention to the unfallen watchers. The third book was written in Hebrew, the Rabbinic Text. All three Enoch books were written between the third century BCE and the second century ACE. The story of Enoch took place in the pre-great flood period some twelve to fourteen thousand years ago. Some have tried to date the section of One Enoch to around the second to first century BC. The researchers also believe the interpretation could mean the Sons of God passage in Genesis 6.

Book One of Enoch also contains the story of angels mated with human females, giving rise to a race of hybrids known as the Nephilim. The term irin usually refers to disobedient watchers who numbered two hundred, of whom their leaders are named. But equally, Aramaic iri ("watcher" singular) is applied to the obedient archangels who chain them that are disobedient, such as Raphael (1 Enoch 22:6).

In the Book of Enoch, the watchers (Aramaic, iyrin) are angels dispatched to Earth to watch over humans. After noticing how beautiful the human women were, the angels started lusting after the earthly women God commanded them to watch over and protect. At the prodding of their leader Samyaza, he encouraged the angels to defect in masse to instruct humanity and procreate among them illicitly. The children produced by the human women and angels were called Nephilim; they grew up as savage giants who pillaged the Earth and endangered humanity.

The angel leader Samyaza and his associates further taught their human charges arts and technologies such as weaponry, cosmetics, mirrors, sorcery, and other techniques that would otherwise be discovered gradually over time by humans, not imposed upon them all at once. Eventually, God allows a great flood to rid the Earth of the Nephilim; that is when God sends Uriel to warn Noah so as not to eradicate humans.

The watchers ended up bound "in the valleys of the Earth" until Judgement Day (Jude verse 6 says, "And the angels which kept not their first estate, but left their habitation, he hath reserved in everlasting chains under darkness unto the judgment of the great day.")

The Book of Enoch listed the chiefs of tens, are as follows: 7. And these are the names of their heads: Shemihazah – this one was their leader; the following are his deputies: Arteqoph, Remashel, Kokabel, Armumahel, Ramel, Daniel, Ziqel, Baraqel, Asael, Hermani, Matarel, Ananel, Setawel, Samshiel, Sahriel, Tummiel, Turiel, Yamiel, Yehadiel, all twenty are their chiefs of tens.

(George W.E. Nickelsburg, 1 Enoch: The Hermeneia Translation, Chapter 6).

The Book of Enoch includes a list of leaders of the two hundred fallen angels who married the women of Earth. This commenced in unnatural union with human women, and these fallen angels taught forbidden knowledge. Some fallen angels are listed in the Book of Raziel (Sefer Raziel HaMalakh), the Zohar, and the Jubilees. To list a few:

- Azazel taught humans to make knives, swords, and shields and how to devise ornaments and cosmetics.
- Gadreel taught the art of cosmetics, using weapons, and killing blows.
- Baraqel taught astrology.
- Bezaliel mentioned to Enoch 1 left out most translations because of damaged manuscripts.

- Kokabiel is a high-ranking, holy angel in the Book of Raziel. In Enoch I, he is a fallen watcher, a resident of the nether realms. He commands 365,000 surrogate spirits to do his bidding.
- Penemue "taught mankind the art of writing with ink and paper" and taught "the children of men the bitter and the sweet and the secrets of wisdom." (I Enoch 69.8)
- Samyaza is one of the leaders of the fall from Heaven.
- Shamsiel, once a guardian of Eden as stated in the Zohar, served as one of the two chief aides to the archangel Uriel (the other aide being Hasdiel) when Uriel bore his standard into battle, and head of 365 legions of angels and crowns prayers, accompanying them to the 5th Heaven. In Jubilees, he is referred to as one of the watchers.
- Yeqon or Jeqon (Hebrew: romanized: Yaqum, "he shall rise") was the ringleader who first tempted the other Watchers into having sex with humans. He had accomplices Asbeel, Gadreel, Penemue, and Kasdaye (or Kasadya), who were all identified as individual "satans."

The account of the Book of Enoch has been associated with the passage in Genesis 6:1-4, which speaks of the Sons of God instead of Watchers. There is a difference in terminology between these two Books, Enoch, and the Old Testament. Did Constantine see these differences in 325 AD? And did he not believe the Book of Enoch? Biblical Scholars debate these elements of the historical biblical accounts still to this day. It could have been clearer at times writing these stories. Angels, as they said, were non-sexual with no gender, but in the Book of Enoch, they were sexual angels able to take human women as wives. Then the Lord said, "My Spirit shall not remain in man forever, since he is but flesh. His days shall comprise one hundred and twenty years." That would mean, as the Lord said, that the Nephilim would only live in the flesh for one hundred twenty years, no matter if they are giants and hybrids of the Fallen Angels. (Wikipedia.org/wiki/Watcher angel)

9

NEPHILIM (BIBLICAL PEOPLE)

In the Hebrew Bible, Nephilim is a group of mysterious beings or people of unusually large size and strength. They lived both before and after the Great Flood. These beings, the Nephilim, were mentioned in Genesis and Numbers and are possibly referred to in Ezekiel in the Bible. The Hebrew word Nephilim is sometimes directly translated as "giants" or taken to mean "the fallen ones." However, as I stated earlier, scholars are still debating the identity of the Nephilim.

Scriptural references

The Nephilim were mentioned in Genesis 6:4 and said to exist just before the Flood account. Which states: The Nephilim were on the Earth in those days – and afterward – when the sons of God went into the daughters of humans, who bore children to them. These were the heroes that were old warriors of renown. If you are confused by this hero-warrior statement about the fallen angels, so am I. Our Lord God did not say they were heroes. He condemned them as disobedient servants of God to be sent into the earth's valleys. The Nephilim again in Numbers 13:32-33 as the Israelites prepared to enter the land of Canaan (the land of milk and honey): So, they brought to the Israelites an unfavorable report of the land they spied out, saying, "The land that we have gone through as spies is a land that devours its inhabitants; and all the people that we saw in it are of great size. There we saw the Nephilim (the Anakites come from the Nephilim), and to ourselves, we seemed like grasshoppers to them. (www.britannica.com/Nephilim)

Some scholars have argued that the "fallen mighty men" in Ezekiel 32:27 are an indirect reference to the Nephilim. The phrase in Hebrew is somewhat ambiguous and misleading. The passage in Ezekiel of a description of the pit of the graves states: And they do not lie with the fallen warriors of long ago who went to Sheol with their weapons of war.

Whereas their swords were laid under their heads, whose shields are upon their bones, for the terror of warriors was in the land of the living. I would interpret this as the Nephilim failed in their conquest at Sheol, and their swords and shields were left on their dead bodies. Who were their enemies who subjected these Nephilim to terror in the land of the living? I am not a Biblical scholar, but it would seem they battled with humans for Earth supremacy. Another cause for this defeat was that God sent his obedient angels to dispatch the Nephilim.

Further Interpretation

Given all this ambiguity in the Genesis passage, there are several interpretations of the relationship between the "sons of God" and the Nephilim. Some scholars have taken the understanding that the sons of God are the fallen angels, with the Nephilim the offspring they produced with human women. This concept is described in the First Book of Enoch, a noncanonical Jewish text, and this idea remains a popular explanation. The Book of Enoch also notes that the Nephilim were giants, which stands to reason about the statement that the spies said the "people of great size" described in the Numbers passage. The confusion about giants being born from human women is a mystery that could only be explained that the fallen angels were supernatural in origin. The other reasonable thought is that it is theologically problematic to think that angels or demons, as good and evil spiritual beings, could reproduce with humans. Angels are supposed to be genderless, as angels were described earlier in this book and stated in the Bible.

A whole new perspective would view this human and fallen angel reproduction idea as simply men who fell away from righteousness and God. Theologians have held that the "sons of God" are a reference to the descendants of Seth, the righteous son of Adam. The Nephilim were members of his bloodline that rejected God. St. Augustine and other Church Fathers held the Sethian view, and Jewish theologians held this view. The Sethian idea also referred to the "daughters of men" as being ungodly women of the bloodline of Cain, Adam's murderous son. If the Nephilim were considered mere humans, their" significant size" would be taken literally or metaphorically, maybe because they were considered great warriors. Getting confusing now, isn't it? Scholars over the millennium still haven't figured the Nephilim origin out. The confusion comes when you consider the books left out of the Bible at the First Council of Nicaea. Like Enoch, Mary Magdalene, Judas, and Thomas that King Constantine in 325 AD told the scribes to leave out the Church's final version of the Bible. (Melisa Petruzzello, www.britanica.com/ Nephilim)

1. Enoch Etiological Interpretation

According to 1 Enoch 7.2, the story is repeated that the fallen angels (Watchers) became "enamored" with human women and had intercourse with them. The offspring of these unions, and the knowledge they were giving, evil human beings and the Earth (1 Enoch 10.11-12). Leaders amongst these angels are Shemyaza and Azazel. They also introduced men to "forbidden arts," and Azazel was rebuked by Enoch for illicit instruction, as stated in 1 Enoch 13.1. According to 1 Enoch 10.6, God sends the archangel Raphael to chain Azazel in the desert Dudael as punishment. It seems Azazel is blamed for the corruption of the Earth. As you read deeper into Enoch, some of the definitions and types of corruption caused by the fallen angels vary from one account to another. Azazyel, as mentioned in 1 Enoch, was blamed for all the corruption of the Earth. Writing these different approaches to the fallen angels allows readers to judge how they see the Enoch books.

The etiological interpretation of 1 Enoch deals with the origin of evil. By blaming the fallen angels for all of mankind's sins and their misdeeds to illicit angel instruction, evil is put on the supernatural aspect from without and not purely on humankind. This idea, in 1 Enoch, differs from that of later Jewish and Christian theology; in the latter, evil is something from within. According to a paradigmatic interpretation, 1 Enoch might be dealing with illicit marriages between priests and women. As evident from Leviticus 21:1-15, priests were prohibited from marrying impure women. This compares the priest to the fallen angels being expelled from Heaven and the priest removed from the altar.

Apocalyptic writings like 1 Enoch reflect a growing dissatisfaction with the priestly establishments in Jerusalem in the 3rd century BC. Biblical scholars believe the Books of Enoch were written in the 3rd century BC, but Enoch's story happened before the great flood of twelve thousand BC. This is passing off where evil originated parallels the Adamic myth regarding the origins of evil. This contrasts with the etiological interpretation, which implies another power besides God in Heaven. Of course, the latter solution poorly fits into monotheistic thought. In Greek mythology, the fallen angels represent creatures that introduced the forbidden arts used by Hellenistic Kings and generals, resulting in the oppression of Jews. What did the ancient scrolls mean in their text? Why are some of the myths of ancient Biblical writings so confusing? Since ancient history is not a precise exact science, we lack Biblical stories' full proof and meanings. They speak of myths throughout Enoch and ancient Greek writings. Is that how we are to interpret these stories through our different perspectives as individuals?

2. Enoch Interpretations

The Second Book of Enoch also contains the concept of fallen angels. This time it talks about Enoch's ascent through the different layers of Heaven. While traveling through the Heavens, he encounters fallen angels imprisoned in the second Heaven.

In the fifth Heaven, however, Enoch meets rebellious angels, here called Grigori, remaining in grief, not joining the Heavenly hosts in song. Strange that at that time, Enoch tried to cheer up the rebellious angels. It seems odd to me; I hope scholars can make sense of this meeting in Heaven by Enoch. Ironically the leader of the Grigori was referred to as Satanail and not Azael or Shemyaza, as in other Books of Enoch.

The narration of the Grigori in 2 Enoch 18:1-7, who went down to Earth, married women, and "befouled the Earth with their deeds," resulting in their confinement under the Earth, shows that the author of 2 Enoch knew about stories in 1 Enoch. The longer recension of 2 Enoch, chapter 29 refers to angels who were "thrown out from the height" when their leader tried to become equal in rank with the Lord's power (2 Enoch 29:1-4), an idea probably taken from Ancient Canaanite religion about Attar, trying to rule the throne of Baal. Later, Christians adopted this usurping of thrones of a higher deity regarding the fall of Satan. In passing down folklore stories from one generation to another, there seem to be similarities between the rise and fall of angels and Satan. The scribes would either add or remove parts of the epic story relevant to their time and reasoning. (Wikipedia.org/wiki/fallen angel)

Jubilees

The Book of Jubilees, an ancient Jewish religious work accepted as canonical by the Ethiopian Orthodox Church and Beta Israel, refers to the Watchers, among the angels created on the first day. This tells me that the Book of Jubilee makes a definite difference between angels and watchers. Watchers were made simultaneously as angels, bringing more confusion about who the Watchers were. In the first Book of Enoch, God commanded the Watchers to come to Earth and instruct humanity. It was only when they copulated with human women that they transgressed the laws of God. These unions brought about demonic offspring, who battle each other until they die, while the Watchers are bound in the depths of the Earth as punishment. Mastema appears as the leader of the evil spirits in this twist of the Book of Enoch. He asks God to spare some of the demons, so he might use their aid to lead humankind into sin. Mastema asks God to leave some demons for him to control; if not, he said he would not be able to execute the power of his will on the sons of men, for great is the wickedness of the sons of men. The Book of Jubilees does not hold that evil was caused by the fallen angels in the first place. The Book of Jubilees seems to have no power independent from God but only acts within his power. These books can become confusing, and you must study each verse to get a reference point of meaning.

Both the (first) Book of Enoch and the Book of Jubilees include the motif of angels introducing evil to humans. (Wikipedia.org)

10

CONFUCIUS

The concept of Heaven (Tian) is pervasive in Confucianism. Confucius had a deep trust in Heaven and believed Heaven overruled human efforts. Confucius also said that he was carrying out the will of Heaven, and Heaven would not allow its servant, Confucius, to be killed until his work was done. Confucius was a Prophet. There are no Confucius gods, and Confucius himself is worshipped as a spirit rather than a god. Community spiritualism and rituals were important in Confucianism, where civic rituals happen. There is still an unresolved debate about whether many people consider Confucianism a religion and a philosophy. It is also disinterested in the supernatural.

Confucius was born in 550 BC in a soldier's family 500 years before Christ.

Confucius honored Heaven as the supreme source of goodness:

The Master said, "Great indeed was Yao as a sovereign! How majestic was he! It is only Heaven that is grand, and Yao corresponds to it. How vast was his virtue?"

Confucius felt personally dependent upon Heaven (VI, xxviii, tr. Legge 1893:193) "Wherein I have done improperly, may Heaven reject me! May Heaven reject me!"

Confucius believed that Heaven could not be deceived:

During the remission of his illness, Confucius said, "Long has the conduct of You been deceitful! By pretending to have ministers when I do not have ministers, whom shall I impose upon? Shall I impose upon Heaven? Is it not better for me to die in the hands of my disciples? I understand that Confucius believed in Heaven and did not believe in ministers to aid him in his trip to Heaven. Only his disciples and Heaven can take him to rest.

Confucius believed that Heaven gives people tasks to perform to teach them virtues and morality. He believed that Heaven knew what he was doing and approved of him, even though none of the rulers on

Earth might want him as a guide. The Master said, "Alas, no one knows me." Zi Gong said, "What do you mean by thus saying – that no one knows you?" Confucius said, "I do not murmur against Heaven. I do not grumble against men. But there is Heaven – that knows me!" The most remarkable saying, recorded twice, is one in which Confucius expresses complete trust in the overruling providence of Heaven. (Tian Wikipedia)

Mozi, another follower of Confucius, said that Heaven is the divine ruler, just as the Son of Heaven is the earthly ruler. Mozi believed that spirits and minor demons exist or at least rituals should be performed as if they did for social reasons, but their function is to carry out the will of Heaven, watching evildoers and punishing them. Mozi taught that Heaven loves all people equally and that each person should love each other equally.

In summation, Confucius was the shortest religion/philosophy to explain, and its interpretation and belief were easy to grasp. No Divinity was mentioned, and no gods participated in this philosophy of Confucius. Confucius and Mozi did not say a monotheistic religion (worshipping one God) like Judaism, Christianity, and Muslim beliefs. They believed that Heaven was instilled with all their spiritual needs and a place of final rest. Only Heaven can ritually judge them. In my search for angels in this belief, I did not find that they took instructions from angels as God's messengers. They believed that each human was responsible for morality and loving one another with only the help of Heaven. This research also surprised this author by not finding God or angels involved in philosophy or religion like Confucianism. Let us keep searching, shall we? (Tian Wikipedia)

The Origin of the Chinese Deity T'ien

The sinologist, Herrlee Creel, wrote a comprehensive study on "The Origin of the Deity T'ien" (1970:493-506), which gives us an overview of this Deity.

For at least three thousand years, it was believed that all revered Chinese T'ien, "Heaven," as the highest deity from time immemorial. This same deity was known as Shangdi, Ti, or Shang Ti. New materials have become available in the present century, especially the Shang inscriptions, making it evident that this was not the case. T'ien is not named in the Shang inscriptions, which instead refer with great frequency to Ti or Shang Ti. T'ien was only with the Chou and was a Chou deity.

Creel refers to the historical shift in ancient Chinese names for "god," from Shang oracles that frequently used di and shangdi and rarely used tian to Zhou bronzes and texts that used tian more frequently. Creel analyzes all the tian and di occurrences meaning "god; gods" in Western Zhou era Chinese classic texts and bronze inscriptions. Some research found that Shi Jing's "Classic of Poetry" has 140 tian and forty-three di or shangdi. Authenticated Western Zhou bronzes (1970:464-75) mention tian ninety-one times and di or shangdi only four times. Upon examining these twenty-six oracle scripts that scholars (like Guo Moruo) have identified as tian "Heaven; god" (1970:494-5), he rules out eight cases in fragments where contextual meaning is unclear. Graphic variants for da "great; large; big" ("great settlement Shang"), as a place name, and four cases of oracles recording sacrifices yu tian (which could mean "to Heaven/God" or at a place called Tian.") Scholars are still working on this ancient Chinese history mystery. From all this information, it is difficult to assume the ancients worshipped Heaven, or "God," at a place called Tian.

This story might highlight a "God" approach by Chinese Kings. Tang of the Shang assembled his subjects to overthrow King Jie of Xia, the infamous ruler of the Xia Dynasty, but the subjects were reluctant to attack. The King said, "Come, ye multitudes of the people, listen to my words. It is not I, the little child [a humble name used by Kings], who dare to undertake what may seem a rebellious enterprise, but for the many crimes of the sovereign of Hsia [Xia], Heaven has given the charge to destroy him. One of the points I made earlier was about

Kings getting their subjects to fight battles for the King's desires using a higher power as their guide. Tang (King) keeps pushing his subjects to attack the ruler of Hsia, calling him an offender of many crimes. As I fear God [Shangdi], I dare not but punish him. Tang tells his people that Hsia has exhausted the strength of his people. It sounds like Tang wants his subjects to follow their moral compass to decide to punish Hsia because he fears Heaven or God if he makes the sole decision.

Still no strong mention of "God," a monotheistic spiritual divine entity in Chinese beliefs. The other fact not seen in the Chinese Beliefs of Tian is no mention of spiritual messengers like angels or watchers. Just a word of "gods," Heaven is the arbiter of their non-spiritual beliefs. This is the reason I wanted to cover all religions or beliefs to look for "God" and Angels in their ancient records. (Tian – Wikipedia)

11

BELIEFS OF ANCIENT INDIA

Samhitas and Brahmanas

India has one of the oldest written and recorded histories of its religious beliefs worldwide. Rich in spiritual beliefs with statues and monuments that show their past in the spiritual realm. It was mentioned in India's written record that Jesus Christ himself visited the northern Provinces of India to attend an advanced spiritual school during his early travels. There is a monument that existed up until recent years that marked Jesus' stay at the school. Jesus was fifteen years old when he traveled to India. The three Wisemen in the Biblical story of Jesus' birth in Bethlehem visited the Christ child to tell Joseph and Mary that Jesus should go on a spiritual pilgrimage. They told them Jesus should attend the northern India spiritual school to increase his spiritual consciousness.

Several texts in India describe Jesus' attendance at the Holy School. Before ending up in India, he traveled by boat to northern Africa, Egypt, and across the Arabic Sea through Arabia. The Holy Men taught him the different forms of spiritualism during his travels. Spiritual Leaders of India led Jesus to his destination at the Holiest of spiritual Schools. There are scholars, and written texts in India that give an account of Jesus' advanced spiritual learning at the school, and some of the gifts of spiritualism he demonstrated to the Masters were also noted.

The Samhitas, the oldest layer of text in Vedas, enumerates thirty-three devas, either eleven each for three worlds, or as twelve Adityas, eleven Rudras, eight Vasus, and two Asvins in the Brahmanas layer of the Vedic texts. Devas are also called angels in other religious disciplines. As translated by Ralph T.H. Griffith; Deities who are eleven in Heaven; who are eleven on Earth; and who are eleven dwelling with glory in mid-air; may be pleased with our sacrifice.

Just like in other religions, these devas (angels) represent the forces of nature, and some represent moral values (such as the Adityas, Varuna, and Mitra), each symbolizing the epitome of specialized knowledge and creative energy, exalted and magical powers (Siddhis). The most referred to Devas in the Rig Veda are Indra, Agni (fire), and Soma, with the "fire deity" called the friend of all humanity. Soma is the two celebrated in a yajna fire ritual that marks major Hindu ceremonies. Savitr, Vishnu, Rudra (later given the exclusive epithet of Shiva), and Prajapati (later Brahma) are Devas gods. Parvati (power and love) and Durga (victory) are some Devis or goddesses. Many of the deities taken together are worshipped as the Vishvedevas. (Deva – Hinduism – Wikipedia)

Important Devas

- Brahma – the deity of creation.
- Vishnu – the deity of preservation.
- Shiva – the deity of destruction and time; associated with fertility and regeneration.
- Ganesha – the deity of new beginnings, wisdom, and luck.

- Hanuman – the deity associated with courage, reverence, and strength/avatar of Shiva.
- Kartikeya – the deity of victory and war.
- Vishwakarma – the deity of architecture.
- Dhanvantari – the deity of doctors and Ayurveda/avatar of Vishnu.

There are seventeen more Devas, but these are the essential Devas that cover much knowledge for humanity. (Deva – Hinduism – Wikipedia)

Henotheism

In Vedic literature, Deva is not a monotheistic God; rather, a "supernatural, divine" concept manifesting in various ideas and knowledge.

This concept of "supernatural" is a form that combines excellence in some respects, wrestling with weakness and questions in other aspects, and heroic in their outlook and actions, and still tied up with emotions and desires. Max Muller states that the Vedic ideas about Devas are best understood neither as polytheism nor monotheism but as henotheism, where gods are equivalent, with different perspectives and different aspects of reverence and spirituality. Deva (Hinduism) – Wikipedia

Ananda Coomaraswamy states that Devas and Asuras in the Vedic lore are like the Olympian gods and Titans of Greek mythology. The Devas represent the powers of light, and the Asuras represent the powers of darkness in Hindu mythology. In Coomaraswamy's interpretation of Devas and Asuras, it is said that these natures exist in each human being, the tyrant and the angel. Like the old story of the devil talking in one ear and the angel speaking in the other ear of a human being trying to get their way. Each person is said to have the best and worst within each person's struggles before choices and one's nature. Devas and Asuras is an eternal dance between these bad or good choices.

In this case, the Titan is potentially an angel, the angel by nature a Titan; the Darkness in actu is Light, the light in potential Darkness; whence the designations Asura and Deva may be applied to the same Person according to the mode of operation. All-powerful beings, good or evil, are called Devas and Asuras in the oldest layer of Vedic texts. They are born from the same father, Prajapati, the primordial progenitor; his sons are envisioned as the Asuras and Devas. They share the same residence (Loka), eat the same food and drink (Soma) together, and have innate potential, knowledge, and special powers in Hindu mythology. As you read this paragraph about Devas and Asuras, you find they were born to the same father. These Devas and Asuras also eat food and drink, whereas other angels in many different religions do not eat or drink. Their father is not "God." It is Prajapati, a human mythological being. I found these apparent differences interesting regarding how different beliefs/religions and Countries record their ancient history.

Classical Hinduism

In Hinduism, Devas are celestial beings associated with various aspects of the cosmos. Devas like Brahma, Vishnu, and Shiva, form Heaven in Hinduism mythology. That statement brings Devas closer to the Heaven aspect and higher powers but not the same as the other religions and beliefs. Everyone starts as an Asura in Hindu mythology, born of the same father. Asuras that don't elevate to Devas stay powerful and obsessed with power, wealth, ego, anger, force, and violence. Devas (Hinduism) (Wikipedia)

Devas are invisible to the human eye. I have always said that I can sometimes feel strange energies around me. It is said that a deva can be detected by those humans who have opened the "Divine eye" (divyacaksus), an extrasensory power that can see beings from other planes. The Divine eye can also pick up voices around them that have cultivated divyasrotra, a power like the human ear. Devas can also construct illusory forms by which they can manifest themselves to the beings of lower worlds. As mentioned, Devas eat and drink but do not require the same sustenance as humans, although the lower kinds eat and drink. (As mentioned earlier) Higher orders of deva shine with their intrinsic luminosity. (Angels in Islam – Wikipedia)

12

WHAT DOES THE BIBLE SAY ABOUT DEMONS?

The Bible tells us that demons are fallen angels who joined Satan in his rebellion against God and were defeated and cast out of Heaven along with Satan (Revelation 12:7-9). Demons are said to this day to serve the devil by leading the world away from God and into sin. Jesus has been said to have banished Satan and his demons into eternal fire. (Dolores Smyth, crosswalk.com)

To understand what demons are, we must look to the ultimate evil spirit himself, Satan. Revelations tell us that Satan was an angel in Heaven, perhaps even a cherub (Revelations 12:7-9). Satan was once an angelic follower of God, but of their own free will, they chose to reject God and become evil. There is no definitive answer as to whether Satan rebelled against God because of his pride or some other reason. We know a war erupted in Heaven in which the archangel Michael and his angels fought against Satan and his followers (Revelations 12:7-9). Satan was defeated along with his fallen angel followers; as their punishment, they all were cast out of Heaven (Revelation 12:9; Luke 10:18). Satan and his evil fallen angels were hurled to Earth and ultimately condemned to hell (Matthew 25:41).

What can Demons do?

Demons continue to serve Satan on Earth by luring mankind away from God. (crosswalk.com)

The Bible warns of Satan's grave threat to humanity by referring to him as "the god of his age" (2 Corinthians 4:4) who prowls the Earth looking for someone to devour (1 Peter 5:8).

The Bible describes demons as: "impure spirits" (Mark 1:27), "deceiving spirits" (1 Kings 22:23), powers of the dark world and the spiritual forces of evil (Ephesians 6:12), and Satan's "angels" (Revelations 12:9). The Bible tells us that Satan and his demons can inflict harm on Earth by:

Possessing people (Matthew 12:22; Mark 5:1-20) and making them do evil (Luke 22:3-4).

Blinding the minds of unbelievers so they cannot see the light of the Gospel (2 Corinthians 4:4).

Deceiving people by disguising themselves as "servants of righteousness" (2 Corinthians 11:14-15).

Promoting false doctrine (1 Timothy 4:1) and performing signs to deceive humans (Revelations 16:14).

Tormenting believers (2 Corinthians 12:7).

How can Christians Resist Evil?

Christians fear becoming possessed by demons since it was a genuine concern in Biblical times. Jesus commissioned his Apostles to spread the Good News, and Jesus gave authority to drive out all demons (Luke 9:1). Some Christian denominations believe in present-day demon possession; others believe practicing Christians cannot be possessed because the Holy Spirit abides in them. Thus, demons cannot take hold (2 Corinthians 1:22). The Bible gives us a clear way to thwart the devil's and demons' efforts to lure us into sin. The best way is by living by the Biblical scriptures steeped in obedience to Scripture. Bible also assures us that if we submit to God and resist evil, the devil and demons will flee from us (James 4-7; Luke 10:17).

The influences of demons can be seen in many places and in the number of things they do. Demons can control minds and inflict possession on a person's cha, changing their anor and controlling their actions. This can also be associated with mental illness in which evil energies might be able to control erratic behavior. They can make people do things they normally would not do. We must wonder if demons take over the criminal mind or if the person was born with mental illnesses. Again, their power is far-reaching but can be exercised within limits. That is why a person should exercise a strong spirituality, and they can make good decisions instead of taking wrong turns in life. The question is, are some people born with mental disabilities without demon involvement? Yes. The Bible speaks of degrees of wickedness among the demons. Jesus said. When an unclean spirit has left its host human, it wanders through waterless regions looking for a new resting place but finds none. (Matthew 12:43-45). (JSTOR Daily)

In the New Testament, the gospels of Matthew, Mark, and Luke begin to equate demons with evil spirits. They also unify the figures of Satan, the devil, and Beelzebul. Luke refers to Satan as "falling from Heaven," while Matthew says, "the devil and his angels." In the second half of the second century CE, Assyrian Christian theologian Tatian fully identified demons as the "arch-rebel" Satan and the fellow angels that followed Satan to his banishment. Could this be true that the Devil and his demon followers are banished from the Earth forever? Could Jesus have rid the world of these evil spirits with his spiritual powers through God? Let us all hope so, which would make demons no more harmful to humans. The author Martin suggests that if we would understand how ancient Jews and Christians viewed angels and demons it "may spark our imaginations to think anew about the cosmos and cosmic demography." (Where Demons Come From – JSTOR Daily)

13

WERE ANGELS INVOLVED IN PLANNING OUR COUNTRY IN THE USA?

T he story of Saint-Germain involved helping forty-nine of our first American Delegates in Philadelphia on July 4th. 1776 in writing the "Declaration of Independence," has always fascinated me. I felt St. Germain and other angels helped our fledgling Country get its start and assisted our forefathers in defeating the British. The history of St. Germain goes back as far as seventy thousand years ago.

The stories from Germany and France say he was an Atlantean Ruler. It was also said that St. Germain was in Germany in 1777 after helping with the Declaration of Independence in 1776, working with Prince Charles of Hesse-Cassel, and collaborating in the study of alchemy. They were both involved with the Masonic Rite of the Strict Observance, which claimed Knight Templar origins for Freemasonry. There is no historical record of Saint – Germain's being active in the craft; Cagliostro later claimed to have received Masonic initiation from him.

St. Germain was called a Templar by Cadet de Gassicourt; Deschamps asserted that Saint – Germain did initiate people into the

Templar Order. Graffer reported that Saint – Germain, in 1776, explained the principles of magnetism to Mesmer, who had already begun to discover magnetism. After Mesmer (in the American Colonies) discussed with Saint – Germain about magnetism, he resorted to entirely attributing it to animal magnetism. More than one writer at that time suspected that Saint – Germain's guiding hand was upon several Masonic and secret spiritual societies whose heads were unknown. Besides being associated with the Frates Lucis and Knights Templar, his name was associated with the Asiatic Brothers, the order of the Strict Observance, which St. Germain found, and the Rosicrucian groups. (The mysterious Stranger in Philadelphia July 4th, 1776/ Be Kind. We are all in this together)

Saint – Germain, the Stranger who gave courage to doubters and sealed the destiny of the new nation – America.

In his Secret Destiny of America, Manly P. Hall refers to the appearance in America before the signing of the Declaration of Independence in 1776 of a mysterious Rosicrucian philosopher, a strict vegetarian who ate only what grew above ground, who was a friend and teacher of Benjamin Franklin and George Washington, and who seemed to have played an essential role in the founding of the new republic.

In my opinion, the story of Saint – Germain is very mysterious. Who was this person? A time traveler? Or an angel that went around countries worldwide to help humankind get a civilized start with their Nations. I feel he behaved like the typical angel not eating much in his eating and drinking mannerisms. He only drank hot tea and not water and was a vegetarian. He was also over six foot four inches tall, just like George Washington. Am I drawing a correlation between the two? Very possible. They were both mysterious and knew each other very well. Nobody saw Saint – Germain entering the building where the Declaration of Independence was signed. Invisibility capabilities like that of angels and disguising as humans like angels sounds like Saint – Germain's mode of operation. Just this author's opinion.

On the day of the Declaration of Independence in Philadelphia on July 4, 1776, Friedenwald said forty-nine Delegates were present in Freedom Hall. But only forty-five would be necessary to sign the Declaration. Seven Delegates were absent. New York's eight-person delegation didn't vote at the time because of the distance of traveling to Philadelphia. The signers' names weren't released publicly until early 1777 when Congress allowed the names of the signers to be attached. The first signature on the Declaration and the one who authenticated the printing was John Hancock. Hence the famous John Hancock signature. He was the first to listen to Saint – Germain's speech with intensity and awe. Then the rest of the Delegates signed the Declaration after Hancock signed it.

Let us go back to the Delegates' initial meeting with a stranger before the signing by Hancock of the Declaration. After Saint-Germain gave his heartfelt speech to the Delegation in the Freedom Hall, explaining that they had no worries about signing the document. He said to sign this document for your freedom even if you lose your head to the British; this Country will thrive and be a great Country. Saint-Germain fell into his seat, exhausted after a twenty-minute speech. Strangely, nobody except for Franklin and Washington knew this stranger, and they were not present at that meeting. Saint-Germain said I would stay on the balcony until you finish writing the Declaration. When you are done, I will read it before I leave, and I am sure it will be an excellent document. The Delegates got carried away by this stranger's enthusiasm and rushed forward after finishing the Declaration of Independence, ready to sign. Saint-Germain looked at the finished document and said you gentlemen did a good job. Now sign this Declaration. As earlier stated, John Hancock jumped for the pen to be the first to sign the Declaration. The rest clambered to get a pen to sign the document, filled with courage and enthusiasm after Saint-Germain gave an incredible speech. After they all signed the Declaration (forty-nine Delegates), they turned to thank Saint-

Germain. Saint-Germain vanished, and no one saw him leave the building. Just when he entered the room before the signing, no one saw him go, not even the Sergeant of Arms. They never saw the stranger again after the signing of the Declaration; he left Philadelphia without being noticed. Strange? No doubt, he was an angel that traveled through time and space.

Interesting Implications in The Stranger's Words

Saint-Germain spoke of the 'rights of man' although Thomas Paine's book by that name was not published until thirteen years later.

He also mentions the "all-seeing eye of God," which was afterward to appear on the reverse of the Great Seal of the new nation. Saint-Germain also helped Washington and Franklin design the first American flag. Before the Declaration was written, it was called "The Grand Union Flag." It had the stripes like the American flag but had a small Union Jack (British Flag) where the stars are located now. Did Saint-Germain help build the America we know today? It sounds like he had a spiritual plan for this Country. "In God, we Trust" is our moral compass in this new Country of "America." Angels like Saint-Germain helped steer us in the right direction of our great fate. Angels were involved with George Washington during the Revolutionary War; we will visit those stories next. (The mysterious stranger on July 4th, 1776 in Philadelphia singing, "Be kind. We are all in this together")

President George Washington's Angels and Visions

The same angel of God that appeared unto Joseph Smith and revealed to him the history of the early inhabitants of America, whose mounds, bones, and remains of towns and fortifications speak of the dust in the ears of the living with the voice of undeniable truth. This is the same angel that presides over the destinies of America and feels a lively interest in all that we do in this Country. This same angel was in camp Washington; by an invisible hand, who was presently in attendance with our founding fathers to conquest and victory; all of this was to open and prepare the way for the Church and Kingdom of God to be established in the western hemisphere. Under the guardianship of this same angel, or prince of America, has the United States grown, increased, and flourished like a sturdy oak tree.

Could this corroborate Sherman, Washington's personal biographer's account? The principal angel in Valley Forge was, of course, described as a woman. But a male angel (or male angels) anointed the land.

As Washington's visions continued, the Angel Moroni hypothesis became more interesting. After the principal angel described to Washington what sounds like another conflict to hit the land – "the thundering of the cannon, clashing of swords, and shouts and cries of millions in mortal combat" – the male angel performed a familiar act that was witnessed by others in the past.

"Son of the Republic," said the female angel, "look and learn." Washington then beheld a male angel and, according to Sherman, told how the angel "placed his trumpet once more to his mouth and blew a long fearful blast." Then Washington instantly said a light, as a thousand suns shone down from above me and pierced and broke into fragments the dark cloud that enveloped America. At the same time, the angel bore our national flag in one hand and a sword in the other. The angel descended from the Heavens, attended by legions of bright spirits. These bright spirits joined the inhabitants of America but immediately took up courage again and renewed the battle. From this author's perspective, this is where Washington was saying the spirits joined Washington's soldiers and gave them strength to renew their battle.

Then once more, Washington saw villages, towns, and cities springing up where he had seen them before. A bright angel planted azure standard he brought amid them. The angel cried loudly: "While the stars remain, and the Heavens send down dew upon the

Earth, so long shall the Union last!" While people are kneeling, said Amen." The biographer could not read this account without thinking of the Biblical prophecy of the angel Moroni found in Revelation 14:6-7: "And I saw another angel fly amid Heaven, and to every nation and kindred and tongue, and people, saying with a loud voice, Fear God, and give glory to him; for the hour of judgment is come: and worship him that made Heaven, and Earth. In this experience (vision), Washington saw that God was responsible for helping him and his army to beat the enemy and to make a great nation – America.

Indeed, the forthcoming Restoration of a new nation had nowhere safe to land. God needed to create an asylum for a new nation and its people. Writing from Valley Forge, Washington knew he was helping God do just that. He declared: "Even if the rest of the world knew it."

George Washington wanted to tell someone about his angelic visitations at Valley Forge before he died. So, he called on journalist Wesley Bradshaw to meet him at Independence Hall – where the signing of the Declaration of Independence happened. Washington started relating the vision his Heavenly visitors gave him, saying there would be more wars in this land. It sounded like the war for Independence, the Civil War, and other conflicts that this great nation would overcome. (Did the Angel Moroni Appear to George Washington? LDS Living)

The darkest period of the Revolutionary War was when Washington had made several reversals, retreating to Valley Forge, where he resolved to pass the winter of 1777. While Washington was talking about those dark days, tears came down his face. He was explaining the deplorable conditions his soldiers had to endure. Washington told the men that they could have lost the battle because of the shortages of food and the cold conditions they had to bear. Washington's feelings toward his soldiers were compassionate, and he would pray to God for his guidance. There were many stories of Washington going to the thicket to pray. This was very true of Washington because he did pray secretly for aid and comfort from God, the interposition of whose Divine Providence brought us safely through the darkest of tribulations.

One day at Valley Forge, Washington remembered well; the chilly winds whistled through the leafless trees. The sky was cloudless, and the sun shone brightly, [Washington] remained in his quarters nearly all afternoon alone. When he decided to come out of his tent, he noticed his face was a shade paler than usual, and he seemed to have something on his mind of more than ordinary importance.

Washington returned to his tent just after dusk; he dispatched an orderly to the officer's quarters mentioned earlier. After speaking to the officer for over a half hour, Washington gazed upon his companion with a strange look of dignity which he alone could command, said to the latter: "I do not know whether it is owing to the anxiety of my mind, or what, but this afternoon, as I was sitting at this table engaged in preparing a dispatch, something seemed to disturb me. Looking up, I beheld, standing opposite me, a singularly beautiful female. So astonished was I, for I gave strict orders not to be disturbed; it was some moments before I found language to inquire the cause of the presence. Several times, I asked this beautiful stranger about this visit, and my mysterious visitor did not answer me. Washington continued by saying there was a strange sensation spreading through me. I would have said more or even arisen from my chair, but the riveting gaze of the beautiful woman before me rendered volition impossible. He said I could not speak or move my body like I wanted to.

While this attractive angelic woman was in Washington's tent, he heard a voice saying, "Son of the Republic, look and learn" at the same time, my visitor extended her arm eastwardly. In this following statement, his angelic guest must have injected visions of traveling over vast continents and looking through clouds. Or was Washington flying with this angelic woman? Washington beheld a heavy vapor at some distance, rising fold upon fold. This gradually dissipated (like clouds?), and he said he looked upon a strange scene. Washington said before I lay spread out in one vast plain all the countries of the world – Europe, Asia, Africa, and America. It sounds like a flight with the angelic woman that she showed Washington the world from high above. "Son of the Republic," said the same mysterious voice as before, "look and learn," At that moment, I beheld another angel, standing or floating in mid-air, between Europe and America.

Was the Angel Moroni One of the Angels Washington Met?

Before we continue with the report on Washington's visions that Sherman (the witness to Washington's visions of angels), the older man Sherman recounts what happened to Washington at Valley Forge five years before. In Salt Lake City on July 4, 1854, Orson Hyde, an ordained Apostle of God, stood in the pulpit in the Tabernacle and boldly declared that the angel Moroni was in the camp of Washington during the Valley Forge angelic event. There was no doubt that Washington was getting his message out and letting people know God was involved in America's victory and freedom for humankind in America. Like other leaders, he felt the same spiritual strength given by God to lead a country to victory, somewhat like Lincoln. Washington had received assurances from the Lord and through his angels about the fate of America. As he led the nation in righteousness, he would be victorious. Washington needed to know this, which gave him the strength to finish and win the Revolutionary War. (Did the Angel Moroni Appear to George Washington? – LDS Living)

On July 4, 1859, Anthony Sherman – one of Washington's soldiers at Valley Forge who was 99 years old – was one of the last remaining veteran soldiers of the Revolution. The angels had a reason for his long life; he was to tell people about Washington's angel visits that helped save our country at Valley Forge eighty-two years prior.

Washington had Angels watching over Him Twenty Years Before the Revolutionary War.

On July 9, 1755, a battle occurred during the French and Indian War, the Battle of Monongahela. During the two-hour battle, twenty-three-year-old Colonel George Washington rode back and forth on the battlefield, delivering the General's orders to other officers and troops. The Indians were told to target officers first. Of the eighty-six British and American officers, sixty-three were casualties. Washington was the only officer on horseback not shot down. Following the battle, Washington wrote a letter to his brother that said:

"By the all-powerful dispensations of Providence, I have been protected beyond all human probability or expectation; for I had four bullets through my coat, and two horses shot under me, yet I escaped unhurt, Washington continued by saying, although death was leveling my companions on every side of me!" (Cleveland corner: George Washington's view of God)

In reading this battle story, Providence spared Washington with four bullet holes through his coat but no bullets in him. For Washington to survive this battle is very interesting in that his angels must have guided him in battle.

Do you know what this is called? A miracle! (Why Washington was impossible to kill – We Are the Mighty)

I (the author) like these stories of Saint-Germain and George Washington because they are both protected by angels or were angels themselves. I wanted to discuss the possibility that this country (America) was founded on the principles of God, who sent his angels to help build a great nation. The mysteries of Washington's miracles continue:

Washington had six of the most lethal diseases of his time. You would likely die if you contracted tuberculosis, dysentery, pneumonia, and simple colds. Not only did Washington survive these illnesses, but he also knew how to inoculate himself, claiming the British tried using the inoculation process as an early form of biological warfare. It was the first mass inoculation by the military. So, was Washington saying he had exposure to this biological warfare that gave him immunity from these illnesses he lived through? MY impression of these stories of Washington's illness recoveries would have to be that the angels cured him, or he knew someone with intelligence above the average intelligence of those days.

Washington was also given bravery and strength from his spiritual Angel visits. During the 1777 Battle of Princeton, Washington rode on his horse as bullets were fired from British rifles at close range. His troops worried about their leader getting shot; he said, "parade with me, my fine fellows; we will have our victory today."

On December 14, 1799, George Washington died at his home after a brief illness and after he lost forty percent of his blood through doctors bleeding him for a cure treatment. It was a strange death, as most claimed during that time. The doctors thought he was felled by what modern doctors believe was a case of epiglottitis, an acute bacterium at the base of the tongue that covers the trachea. (Wikipedia)

Benjamin Franklin's Connections

Benjamin Franklin was never the President of America, which goes against most peoples' beliefs. Franklin worked on the Declaration of Independence in 1775 with George Washington and three other Delegates. John Hancock (the principal signer) of the Declaration of Independence did not like the original Declaration of Independence. He almost rewrote the document because he was unhappy with Franklin's written direction. Hancock, with other Delegates, edited the original document at the 1776 Freedom Hall meeting with forty-nine other Delegates on July 3rd and the fourth. Benjamin Franklin's main job was being an Ambassador to France, and he owned a printing company that mostly printed poetry. What does Franklin's involvement with Washington and the Declaration of Independence have anything to do with angels and the Divine? (Wikipedia)

Benjamin Franklin knew George Washington very well and the mysterious stranger, Saint-Germain, who miraculously convinced forty-nine Delegates to finish writing the Declaration and sign it. Franklin met Saint-Germain first, and he and Washington spoke about their plans for a new nation before July 1776. Previously I stated that Saint-Germain could be an angel traveling on Earth for two thousand years. It is also said that Saint-Germain initiated Washington and Franklin into the Knights Templar higher order. Saint-Germain was also a Mason and brought Washington and Franklin into the Masonic Order. This shows a deep connection between the three of them, and this would tell me they knew angels were helping them build a strong nation. Hence, the angel connection of our founding fathers.

Even though Benjamin Franklin was not a Christian in his religious beliefs, he did believe in God. His family raised him with the Deism beliefs in the Enlightenment philosophy that God was real. Deism, from the Latin term, means (God) and is solely based on rational thought without any reliance on any revealed religions or religious authority. In a sense, they believed God's existence is revealed in nature. Deism was an intellectual and spiritual movement in the 1800s and early 1900s. Deism started in England and France in the 17th and 18th centuries. Franklin was in France, where many Deists were located. Franklin reinforced his beliefs there in France while being an ambassador. Do Deists believe in angels and demons? Yes, most of them did believe in angels. Thomas Paine and Thomas Jefferson were also deists. Angels were not out of the question with these early founders. This author believes they all had secrets and pacts with the angels in helping to build a nation for God – America. Today, the Deist's beliefs would fit the Unitarian Church's religious beliefs. Also, in this modern time, deism is not publicly talked about. It would be a more private and personal belief. (Deism Wikipedia)

President Abraham Lincoln and Angels

President Lincoln was always aware that he had guardian angels since his youth; he said only once did he ask for their help – and that was when he was most afraid. Lincoln could remember the day and the hour that an angel came through for him during his fears.

Most of us know three names of the significant angels – Gabriel, Rafael, and Michael. Each had a different gift and talent – to announce, protect or defend. Lincoln said his faith has helped him to understand that angels hover when we human beings are challenged, in trouble, or most in need – hovering so quietly until we are aware of their presence.

Abraham Lincoln knew about angels. He spoke of them as creatures with the power and grace to intercede for us, assist, and guide us in our most challenging times. Lincoln's toughest time was on March 4, 1861, when he was newly elected president of the United States.

Lincoln knew he was now the president of a country about to go to war – civil war. In his first inaugural address to the nation, he told the people that our country was on the brink of civil war. Lincoln spoke with bold realism about the country's unsettled national mood and division. Lincoln's words bespoke fear, division, anger, judgment, and national shame. He was speaking positively in his speech when he said that when this terrible war would be over, we Americans would find a way to unite again. He felt strongly about reconciliation in the future. It was almost like Lincoln was foretelling the future with the guidance of his guardian angels. Also, this speech about a divided nation sounds like history repeats itself, like what our country is experiencing today, 2022.

Lincoln said we are not enemies, but friends, who have differences. Our passion as a country may have strained us, but it must not break our bonds of compassion with our fellow citizens. Lincoln goes on to make a strange comment when he said the mystic chords of memory would bring a chorus of harmony to our Union. This is when again touched, as they surely will be, by the BETTER ANGELS OF OUR NATURE." We can allow for several theories to this statement about angels. Was Lincoln saying that bad angels are bringing us the evil of war and that the good angels will return us to a Godly nation again? The country was not yet one hundred years old, and a brutal civil war was just around the corner that would cause a tremendous loss of life. Lincoln thought war this bad could be forgiven or forgotten between the North and the South – brother against brother.

Lincoln understood the destruction of war. Still, he reminded his hearers that in each of us, though filled with anger and hate now, there was a "BETTER ANGEL" who could reach out to us when it was time for healing. It was an act of faith on Lincoln's part – faith in God and the American people. A speech that could help us in our troubled country and world. If ever we needed healing with our division and anger, it is now. Jon Meacham, a Pulitzer Prize-winning historian, implores us to focus on the "BETTER ANGELS OF OUR NATURE." This was the fall of 2020 when Meacham made this statement. Meacham reminds us of times in our country, like Lincoln's time when our country has seen very troubling times. Political wrath and hatred in our country – times that "tried men's souls." Meacham went on to say it is a "tragic element of history." Every advance must contend with the forces of reaction. Such is the complexity and imperfections of the democracy on our planet. (Center for Spiritual Development – By Sister Eileen McNerney, CSJ)

No one knows how Lincoln first encountered the phrase "better angels." A possible source of Lincoln's insight into that phrase, most likely: is William Shakespeare's play Othello, written in 1603. Othello murders his wife, Desdemona, accusing her of adultery.

> "Poor Desdemona! I am glad thy father's dead:
>
> Thy match was mortal to him, and pure grief – Shore his old thread in twain: did he live now? This sight would make him do a desperate turn; Yea, curse his BETTER ANGEL from his side. And fall to reprobation."

Did Lincoln read Shakespeare? Nobody knows. Shakespeare in one of his sonnets in 1599, Shakespeare similarly tells of us "two spirits" that are "both from me" – a "better angel" that is "right fair" and a "worse spirit" that tempted my better angel. Thus "would corrupt my saint to be a devil. For Lincoln, the "better angels of our nature" are those civic and patriotic qualities, shaped by shared memory, which permit us, even in times of national fracturing, to swell the chorus of the union. It might have been that Lincoln and Shakespeare that "better angels" were neither individual people nor supernatural beings but instead aspects of human temperament. From what I wrote earlier in this book, Lincoln felt he had a guardian angel as a child and through his presidency. Other historians think of the concept of "better angels" as admirable aspects of temperament or aspirations toward what is good. Edward Bulwer-Lytton, in about 1839, for example, prefigures Lincoln exactly when he yearns for "the better angels of the human heart." ("Better Angels" In our Past – The American Interest)

Lincoln spoke of God but never said he refused Christianity. As a young man, he lacked faith and did not give the Bible much thought. Later in life, during his first years as President, he commented on the abundance of dreams in the Bible. He asserted, "if we believe the Bible, we must accept that in the old days, God and His angels came to men in their sleep and made themselves known in dreams." That was an answer he put to his wife; Lincoln admitted that he did not believe in dreams, but he continued saying as he alluded to a recent dream. This dream, he said, "has haunted me ever since." His wife insisted that he tell her the dream he had that was so profound. Lincoln said, "about ten days ago," he had gone to bed late after staying up "waiting for important dispatches from the front. "As he began to dream, he experienced "a death-like stillness about me." Hearing subdued sobs, Lincoln walked downstairs in search of the "mournful sounds of distress" but encountered no living person until he entered the East Room, where he found "a sickening surprise": a covered corpse resting on a catafalque, surrounded by soldiers, with mourners gazing at the body and weeping. "Who is dead in the White House?" I demanded of one of the soldiers, "Lincoln related in Lamon's account, "The President" was his answer; an assassin killed him!" Lincoln stated that he awoke soon after a "loud burst of grief from the crowd," Lincoln did not sleep again that night due to the dream, and "he has been strangely annoyed by it since." Lincoln insisted to Lamon that the corpse in the catafalque, later, was not him but that of George Washington. A political scientist Dwight G. Anderson speculated that the dead president in the dream was George Washington, and Washington's assassin was Lincoln himself. From Anderson's perspective, it "provided Lincoln with an imaginary father whom he both emulated and defied," which, as Anderson continues, "provided the psychological basis for Lincoln's haunting guilt, "and it provided the psychological basis for Lincoln's re-foundation of political authority in the United States. This is a new concept about Lincoln's dream, but I take this as a conjecture because Lincoln's dream did come to fruition. It happened as he dreamed it that faithful night. Lincoln was assassinated and was in the catafalque. (Teachinghistory.org)

To reinforce the belief that Lincoln saw himself lying dead in the White House Rotunda. It was not the first time Lincoln "saw" his death. Soon after his election in 1860, he would see a double image of his face reflected in a mirror in his Springfield, Illinois home. One was his "real" face, the other a pale imitation. Lincoln's wife, Mary, was a superstitious person, but she did not see the double images and was deeply troubled by her husband's account of the incident. As they say, Lincoln's wife, Mary Todd Lincoln, had her premonitions of being a superstitious person or psychic today. She prophesied that the sharper image of Lincoln was an indication that he would complete his first term as president. The faint, ghostlike image was a sign, she said, that he would be renominated for a second term but would not live to complete. Both Lincoln and Mary had premonitions of futuristic events in the White House. The angels communicated with them because their stress about the Civil War heavily burdened them. Angels help in distressful moments, as Lincoln said earlier in his life, which seemed to feel like angelic involvement. Even though Lincoln would meet his end, the angels thought he served his divine purpose in life.

This incident occurred only a few days before the assassination of President Lincoln. Yet, within Lincoln's monologue, he related at one point that the dream happened "the other night" and ten days ago." This is where Lincoln dreamt of lying in State at the Capital Building, dead. This was during the period between March 24, 1865, and April 9, 1865, when this dream happened. Lincoln said he was at the front lines of the battles rather than the White House when he had this eventful dream. In addition, there was no contemporaneous account of the dream following the assassination. NO writers of the time mentioned the voluminous writings of the period; not even Mary Lincoln, Lamon, his staff member, or anyone else mentioned

Lincoln's dream. Despite these seeming inconsistencies, the Fehren-bachers note that Lamon's account of the dream has been quoted as fact by numerous respected authors. This author believes Lincoln had angels speaking to him and guiding him to his destiny. As Lincoln would say, "angels guard over you during times of distress and troubles." This mainly was the consciousness of Lincoln that held and bared a heavy heart from all the carnage of the civil war. (Teachinghistory.org)

14

EGYPTIAN ANGELS AND BELIEFS

Most researchers have difficulty identifying the exact Egyptian God they represent to the archangels. The confusion is because the Egyptians had a God for everyday activities; all animals and humans had different representations of Egyptian gods. They detailed male and female Gods for similar domains. To further complicate matters, the crescent moon has a different meaning from the full moon, and the planet Venus in the morning (morning star) is not the same as the evening star (Venus). Atum was the sun, Ra, but in his evening aspect, he was different in meaning.

In Pauline Art, Archangels are neither male nor female, like in other religious depictions. In Egyptian art, the Archangels appeared as female-to-male petitioners and male-to-female petitioners. This belief could resemble the Christian, Judaism, and Muslim visions of angels as those religions said angels had no gender but might have been changing to human forms to communicate with humans in distress.

This summarized list of Archangels from the Egyptian God's primary function dominion and the seven Archangels of the ancient world governance are matched to these descriptions. This list gives the reader an idea of the comparisons intended to guide the reader to the appropriate Egyptian God/Archangel.

Egyptian God	Symbolizes	Related Archangel
Aah	God of the Moon	Gabriel
Amun & Amun-Ra	Amen and Imen	Sachiel
Anhur (Anhert, Onouris, Onuris)	A warrior invoked against both human and animal	Samael
Anubis (Anpu)	Jackal, head God, Shepherd the dead to judgement	Azrael
Aten	Sun God – Akhenaten	Michael
Atum (Tum or Tem)	Evening Aspect of Sun God Ra	Michael
Auf (Efu and Ra)	Aspect of the Sun God Ra	Michael
Geb	United with sister Nut. Representative of Earth God	Lumiel
Hathor (Athor)	Daughter of Ra, aspect of Isis	Gabriel
Heket	Goddess of childbirth/fertility	Gabriel
Horus	God of the Sun – son of Osiris	Michael

Others in Archangel groups:

Egyptian God	Archangel
Isis, Nut	Anael
Khons or Khuns	Gabriel
Meskhenet	Gabriel
Nekhbet	Gabriel
Nepthys	Cassiel
Osiris (Marduck)	Cassiel
Ra	Michael
Sekmet	Michael
Seshat	Raphael
Set (Seth)	Lumiel
Thoth (Tehuti)	Raphael

The Egyptian God we most often hear about in this shortened list is Thoth, the God of wisdom. Horus, God of the sun. Ra the sun God, and son of Nut. Isis, the Goddess of fertility, sister of Osiris. And

Osiris, the God of the underworld. There are twenty-two Egyptian gods with Archangels in the above list. Most scholars of ancient Egyptian history need to conclude if these accurately compare gods and Archangels. (Magical Cornucopiaa)

The Angels of Thoth

The followers of Osiris believed in material Heaven, and now we must locate where Heaven was situated. A passage in the text of Unas {line 191 ff. the angels of Thoth, and ancient ones, and the Great Terrifier, who cometh from the Nile River, Hap and Ap-uat, who cometh forth from Ap-uat, are called upon to witness that the mouth of the king is pure because he eats and drinks nothing except that upon which the gods live. The text says, "Ye have taken Unas with you, and he drinketh that which ye drink, he liveth as ye live, he dwelleth as ye dwell, he is powerful as ye are powerful, and he saileth about as ye sail about"; thus, the Heaven where Unas lived after the death was in a boat.

The text continues, "Unas has netted {fowl and fish with the net in Aaru, Unas hath possession over the waters in Sekhet-Aanru, of the later Recensions of the Book of the Dead. The land was divided into several districts; the chief was called Sekhet-Heptep, i.e., "Field of Peace, and was presided over by the god Sekhet-Heptep. In the waters of Aaru or Sekhet-Aaru, Ra purified himself of beings. His Heavenly life here also dwelt in the three classes of beings: Akhemu-seku, Akhemu-Betesh, Akhema-Sesh-emau, and Akhemu-Sesh-emau three classes of celestial bodies or beings who were never diminished or melt away, or decay. This text speaks of celestial bodies or beings, Heavenly life, and beings who never diminish or melt away. The typical angel we discussed in this book talks about the same attributes as angels in other religions. They never diminish, or decay and are referred to as celestial beings. Egyptian terminology differs immensely from other languages, and their belief systems are similar, but as described in text and drawings, they are nearly the same concept of angels. (Egypt Gods – Angels of Thoth)

Kimbas Angels, say I did not realize there were "Angels" in Egyptian culture until I started to read about the deities in Egyptian Mythology and Pantheon when you look up Isis in one of the angel reference books. There Isis was listed in the angel book, to my surprise. Isis is the daughter of Geb and Nut-Sister, Osiris's wife and Horus's mother. Isis is one of the most widely accepted divinities to be worshipped outside of Egypt as well as inside. Isis symbolizes Motherhood, Nurturance, Sovereignty, and stability to her people. Her name is included in many incantations. "In some traditions, she is considered a Seraph." Isis is also compared to an angel, like a Seraph in the text of the angel book. When Isis manifests herself in angel form, it is usually with feathered wings that spread to enfold her worshipers in unity(sleep). Isis also acts the same way as the angel of death. "The line between angels and gods in polytheistic religions, especially in ancient Egypt, was thin, and the representation of winged figures was common." As we discussed earlier, most religions do not accept the idea of a female angel, nor that they have feathered wings. Since angels can shapeshift into whatever their subject wants to see, the angel will make themselves accommodate their targeted human's idea of an angel. (Quora)

Other beings considered to be associated with being "angelic" kind are:

Horus is the divine source of sovereignty and the son of Isis and Osiris. In his manifestations, "Horus of Behtet" reveals himself as a solar disc (halo) with feathered wings. Hence, this story made the halo popular amongst religious followers of angelic people or beings. Having a halo over their heads means that they are divine beings.

The Goddess Nut is the mother of Isis and Osiris and is an aerial goddess of the sky and wind. Most of the time, she is represented by outstretched wings folded around her body. Again, it depicts her as an angelic being like her daughter Isis.

Another example of Egyptian angels is Chaldea Michael; he was considered the angel of the Last Judgement and the "weigher of souls." Being in this role, he was considered a descendant of Anubis. Anubis is a popular figure in Egyptian artwork on the walls of the Tombs of the dead. Anubis is a jackal-headed deity that presides over the judgment of the dead. He is also a protector of mortuaries.

Khonsu (one of the Egyptian gods) is known as the Moon God. He has been known as the divinity invoked in exorcisms and rites of healing. All these Egyptian deities remind us of all the other ancient religions with similar characteristics of angelic beings. Khonsu is depicted as a two-headed falcon with a solar disc (halo) and a set of four feathered wings.

"The idea of unique angelic species probably derived ultimately from influences of Egyptian, Sumerian, Babylonian, and Persian views of supernatural beings. This interaction of ideas produced the familiar image of winged messengers of God. The question is, did all these ancient people see the same angelic beings since they are so close in characteristics and similarities? Angels last for eternity and have no distance or time barriers they cannot navigate. It is possible that folk-lore stories were passed down about these experiences from one culture to another over long periods. (Angels in their art – Quora)

Egyptians could export their phenomenal religion and culture through their far-reaching trade links. Egyptian Mythology is the accumulation of myths derived from ancient Egypt from four thousand BCE to thirty CE. Cleopatra's death marked the end of the last of Egypt's Ptolemaic sovereign. In Egyptian writing and art, myths occur – in short stories and religious materials such as ritual text, hymns, funerary texts, and temple decorations. Most of these artists or texts are fragmented, making it challenging to interpret full accounts. Both Greek philosophers Plato and Pythagoras are believed to be inspired by the belief of Egyptians in reincarnation. The Romans also saw an interest in Egyptian mythology and culture and were broadly accepted, as did other civilizations.

To the Egyptians, humanity's existence was believed to be only a tiny part of the journey of eternity. Deities and supernatural agents (angels) coordinated and ruled over the voyage of life and death. In studying more than the great building projects for which the Egyptians were famous, I can see the interest in the Egyptian's beliefs being the initial starting point of most religious practices and beliefs. The similarities between Egyptian beliefs and other faiths seem evident through different cultures' acceptance. In my studies of Egyptian deities – angels seem to be some undeniable similarities with angel descriptions and beliefs.

According to the historian Bunson:

"Heh, called Huh, was one of the original gods of the Ogdoad (the eight deities worshipped during the old Kingdom, 2575-2134 BCE) at Hermopolis and represented eternity – the goal and destiny of all human life in Egyptian religious beliefs, a stage of existence in which mortals could attain everlasting bliss (86)."

The Egyptians knew that life on Earth was part of the eternal journey; it was an introduction to something bigger – eternity. The concept of the afterlife for Egyptians was a mirror world of one's life on Earth – one's life in Egypt. If one wanted an afterlife, one would have to live life correctly. One must follow Jesus' teachings and live by the ten commandments in Christianity. Live a good moral life here on Earth to go to Heaven and be with Jesus. The Christian religion states that you can only get to Heaven through Jesus. The Egyptians believed in similar moral traits to go to eternity. There are probably more coincidences between Egyptian beliefs and other religions, but their traditions were handed down through storytelling. Passed-down stories and beliefs explain why little detail of the myths exist; every Egyptian that lived in that ancient period knew about the legends. Many texts and artwork have not survived thousands of years of wear and damage. Only a few of these sources remain recognizable to the current times. Egyptian Mythology – Stephen Weaver)

Isis

The gods held significant leverage over the ordinary people in ancient Egyptian society. They were creators of the cosmos and set the order for the people and the rule of laws. The gods and goddesses had their cults separated from the commoners. Egyptian people held rituals and sacrifices for the gods to appreciate their deity supremacy. Isis, as mentioned, was the most powerful of deities or angels of Egyptian culture. Her magical powers were so great that Osiris or Ra could not match her skills. She was loved and worshiped by all social strata. Isis had a close link to Kings and Kingship. Initially, Isis was an obscure goddess without temples consecrated to her, but she grew famous during the advance of the dynastic age. She became one of the chief deities of ancient Egypt. Her cult of Isis spanned dominions as far distant as the Greco-Roman world, the Roman Empire, and Afghanistan. Isis was the ideal wife and mother who was a stout supporter of her husband, Osiris. Maybe jumping thousands of years ahead in modern times, the name Isis still exists in the Middle East but in a more terroristic way. I am sure Isis would disapprove of her name being associated with killing in today's climate. Isis was a nurturer, not a killer of people.

According to ancient Egyptian text sources, Seth was envious of the god of Egypt, Osiris (Isis' husband), and contrived a plan to kill him.

Seth made a wooden chest the size of Osiris as he measured him before his planned murder. He did this in front of a group of people and played a game that involved other people trying to fit in the chest. Seth knew Osiris would fit perfectly because he measured him in his sleep. When he got into the chest, Seth locked it, took the chest with Osiris in it to the river Nile, and threw him in. After killing Osiris, Seth was crowned the Pharaoh of Egypt.

The widow (Isis) set out to find Osiris' corpse and found it at Byblos by a tree. She brought the body back to Egypt. Seth learned of Isis' finding of her husband's body, and he searched and found his body himself. He cut Osiris' body into pieces so nobody would recognize him. It was written that Seth cut the body into fourteen pieces and spread it all over Egypt so Isis would not find Osiris' body.

The persistent Isis was undeterred by the challenge of finding all the parts of her husband's body. With the help of her sister Nephthys, Isis transformed into a bird to see the land from above to locate all the pieces of the body. She collected all but one part of Osiris' body parts but one: his genitals. Unfortunately, a fish had feasted on that organ, and she could not recover that part. Isis replaced the genitals with a golden phallus to make Osiris' body whole again.

Osiris' cut-up body and Isis finding the body were strange enough but what followed had to be a supernatural procedure. Isis used her magical powers to stitch up his body with bandages, transforming him into a mummy, neither dead nor alive. With the help of Thoth's magic, she bore him a son, Horus, after nine months. Then Osiris became the ruler of the dead after being condemned to the underworld. Osiris' demise and reincarnation were revived annually through rituals. To this author, the story of Isis is fascinating because conceiving a baby (son) from a dead man is a miraculous event. What magic did Thoth know to bring life from a dead Osiris to make it possible to impregnate Isis? Were these two Isis and Thoth angels with supernatural powers? These stories happened hundreds of years before Christianity even started. But the stories from Egypt sound vaguely familiar to the miraculous birth of Jesus. Angels were also involved in Jesus 'conception, with Mother Mary being inseminated by supernatural angels.

Isis and Her Son Horus

At Khemmis, Isis bore Horus. She fled to the distant parts of Egypt with her newborn to escape Seth's rage. Horus was very much in danger of many perils. A poisonous scorpion once bit Horus, and Isis used her magical skills to heal him. What magic were they talking about in this story of Horus and Isis? Could Isis have been more knowledgeable and ahead of her time? Supernatural healing usually is from an angel and heals through God's spiritual power. Isis protected her son Horus very diligently throughout his childhood. Isis wanted her son Horus to grow up to be a man, seek vengeance on his father's murderer, and claim the throne. It was the role she played in guarding her son that she earned the title "goddess of protection." (Egyptian Mythology - Stephan Weaver)

The Inspiration of Isis on Christianity

The portraits of Isis breastfeeding her newborn Horos inspired many Christian paintings of the Virgin Mary with her baby Jesus Christ. There are other influences passed down to Jesus and Christianity stories. As mentioned, a halo above the deities' heads that Christianity adopted as their divine entities are displayed in their artwork. When Thoth performed magic to create Isis, a son from her dead husband Osiris's body, that depicted a miracle of birth like Mother Mary; the angels performed the gift of Jesus' inception while Mary was a virgin. Could this be the same supernatural angel forces at work? Horos and Jesus were both Kings in their rites, which makes the story similar. Both Mother Mary and Isis were from a royal bloodline with past Kings and Queens in their lineage. Isis and Mother Mary are worshipped as female religious leaders and were part of a miraculous spiritual event, making them the same historically honored throughout history. Both Horos and Jesus had their battles with overcoming tremendous obstacles. This author is not comparing religions like Christianity with Mythology, just showing the coincidences between the two cultures.

Horos

Horos turned out in his manhood to be an Egyptian deity of kingship and the sun. Horos was also depicted as the god of war, hunting, Upper Egypt, Light, and the same protection characteristics his mother Isis possessed and passed down. Horos was also described as a falcon; he had a right eye that was deified as the sun (morning sun), symbolizing power and epitome. Horos' left eye was the moon (evening star), representing the power of healing.

The Battle of Horos with Seth

The dates written on the walls of the ancient Egyptian building structures indicate that the Horos and Seth battles began around (2925 – 2775 BCE) some have dated these occurrences to happen around (2400 BCE). The artwork and wall drawings are not concise because the story was passed down from generation to generation. Mythology also said that the deities lived several hundred years, making these years possible. These two, Seth and Horos, fought for over one hundred years for kingship over Egypt. They were seen as gods of Egypt, with Horos, the god of Upper Egypt, and Seth, the god of lower Egypt. Horos emerged as the victor not because of a battle triumph but because he acquired the most votes from other gods. He became to be known as the new King of Egypt. During their long physical battle, both were severely injured by their fighting but were mended and healed over time. Earlier in this book, I wrote that angels lived for thousands of years, that is, some angels. Other angels live eternally and never die. If these stories are mythology, they sure indicate details that would subscribe to angels' characteristics of living for long periods and being able to heal themselves. These Egyptian deities also created life like the angels could through supernatural means.

Anubis

Anubis (or Anpu) was the ruler of death, the underworld, and the funeral god. Anubis was the child of Seth and Nephthys, who was never told of the secret of his birth father. He was the adopted son of Isis and Osiris. It was claimed that Isis fooled Seth into making love to her to create Anubis. Isis disguised herself as Nephthys, the wife of Seth, to fool him. Hence, the adopted son was Isis' real son by natural means. This author also sees the same magical powers of Isis and her sister as being able to change bodies as the angels do. The reason for further examining the Egyptian culture for deity and angel similarities. A jackal or a man with a head of a jackal was often the illustration of Anubis. Anubis held a flail, usually held in his arm's crook, and a fetish. Anubis developed the art of embalming with his first body of Osiris; he was accredited with the creation of the craft. (Egyptian Mythology – Stephan Weaver)

The Hall of Truth

If a person at physical death manages to circumvent all the obstacles and passes through all the challenges, he/she will be escorted to the "Hall of Truth." When the deceased reached the "Hall of Truth," they would be asked to swear that he/she did not commit the forty-two sins, also known as the "Negative Confession."

1. I have not sinned.
2. I have not committed robbery with violence.
3. I have not stolen.
4. I have not slain men and women.
5. I have not stolen grain.
6. I have not purloined offerings.
7. I have not stolen the property of the gods.
8. I have not uttered lies.
9. I have not carried away food.
10. I have not uttered curses.
11. I have not committed adultery.
12. I have made none to weep.

Does this list sound familiar? All these sins were based on the principles of the Egyptian culture a thousand years before the ten commandments that Moses brought forth from Mount Sinai that God gave him around the thirteenth century BCE to the eighth century BCE; scholars are still not sure of the date. This story is in the

Judea Christian Bible in chapters of Exodus and Deuteronomy. Moses carried two stone slabs with God's written commandments. If you read the Egyptian list of commandments, they are more in-depth than Moses' ten commandments. Again, similarities between Egyptian religious views and Christian principles. Both lists of sins were to help people follow better morals to get to Heaven or the Egyptian Afterlife. In the "Book of the Dead," it was also written that they would weigh the deceased's heart to finalize the decision to let people go to the afterlife. (Stephan Weaver – Egyptian Mythology)

15

DO THE NEPHILIM STILL LIVE ON EARTH UNDERGROUND?

The Nephilim, the Bible's story of the fallen angels in the Book of Genesis "in the beginning." In Genesis, the story says that the children conceived by the earthwomen by the fallen angels were evil giant beings called Nephilim. Is it possible they still live underground, hiding from humans? It was said that the giant Goliath that David slayed was a Nephilim in the Biblical story of "David and Goliath." Were the Nephilim around during those years, and do they still exist in hiding?

There might be historical evidence that the Nephilim were left behind worldwide. Llandudno (Northern Wales), a coastal village with an ancient copper mine, is located two hundred meters above the Irish Sea level. It has ancient mining sites where artifacts of enormous size have been unearthed. Nine subterranean levels exist in that mining location, and more than one thousand seven hundred tons of copper have been extracted. It was an incredible feat if we think about the community of the time that did not have modern technological tools to accomplish this enormous work. At least not the same machinery we have today. The heaviest hammer that men use today weighs about 9 Kg, but the most used are the 4.5 Kg hammers. Let's imagine a 9 Kg hammer of three hundred percent, and we would obtain a tool of twenty-seven Kg, which, to be maneuvered, should consist of a handle of close to three meters and a metal head as big as a cinder block. (thecomradegeneral.wordpress.com)

Nephilim Today

Isaiah, the Biblical Prophet, tells us that the ghib-bore' is coming. The ghib-bore are the Nephilim, the children of fallen angels, the Giants. When are they coming? On the Day of the Lord approaches, Nephilim will be seen on the Earth. Are you ready for this? It happened before, and it will happen again. The thing that hath been is that which shall be, and there is no new thing under the sun. (Ecc 1:9) Christ explained in Matt. 24:37 to his disciples that the day of his return would resemble the days of Noah and the great flood.

The great Flood is a prerequisite to the understanding of the prophetic implications. This is the Lord's prediction regarding His second coming. The second coming will be in times like Noah's end-of-world flood. In the Gospel of Matthew and the Gospel of Luke, Jesus tells his Disciples that the last days will be filled with iniquity, sin, and licentiousness that deeply grieved the Lord. In Genesis six, in the days of Noah, there were Giants on the Earth. These Giants, or "Nephilim" in Hebrew, are believed to be the offspring of earthly women. Genesis 6:4 claims these Nephilim were the fallen angels.

God has been restraining these "sons of God" who sinned with the daughters of men. The end time, in this sense, is a restoration of Noah's day (Matt. 24:37) in its major features. God will stop restraining their appearance in our realm (2 Thess 2:6), and the Nephilim will return to earth.

The Nephilim could use the false flag attack approach upon their return to Earth. They or their children of the Nephilim will disguise themselves as UFO aliens and preach that they seeded life and guided its progress on Earth, thus hoping to make all religions unbelievable to humans and obsolete. This concept of taking credit for human progress on Earth foreshadows the coming of the antichrist and his false prophet required to take control over the planet. This UFO aliens' invasion was not stated in the Bible or expressed by Christ. Just a theory posed by CK Quarterman (Nephilim Today). In his opinion, that could happen in our modern destruction of the Earth, and comparing Noah's time in history to ours, the aliens could have been with the Nephilim. Jesus did foretell the return of the Nephilim and that we should look out for the Nephilim. What would they look like? How will we recognize them? Do they look like us humans? They may not have wings like angels and six toes and fingers. Some experts say that the Nephilim (fallen Angels) strive to weed out this genetic trait to look more human. (CK Quarterman – Nephilim Today)

The Giant of Kandahar, Afghanistan

Steven Quayle spoke of an occurrence, still classified by the US Government, in his popular Radio Show "Coast to Coast": the events allegedly happened in 2002 in a desert part of Afghanistan when a U.S. Army squad went missing. A Special Ops Task Force was sent to find out what happened. The Special Ops team walked along a ragged mountainous trail and arrived at a large cave entrance. Pieces of destroyed military equipment were scattered about the clearing in front of the cave. When the task force entered the cave to explore its recesses, thirteen feet tall, red-headed, six-digit, double-toothed humanoids emerged and attacked them. According to the survivors (witnesses), the giant pierced one of the soldiers with a long spear killing him.

Before the rest of the Squad could react with firepower, the soldier was killed instantly by the Giant's spear before the Squad could take the Giant down. The Squad fired at the Giant's face for thirty seconds straight to bring the Giant down. It was said that after the Squad leader called in for reinforcements and a helicopter to help them fight these Giants, they were shaken to the core by their fellow soldier's death. The Ops team was at a loss at how huge this Giant was and how fast he could move. The body of the Giant was placed in a large web net hauling basket and transferred to a secret location in the USA for study. Based on Quayle's story, L.A. Marzulli succeeded in identifying and interviewing one of the members of the Task Force who saw and shot – the "Giant of Kandahar." This event's name became known to the soldiers in Afghanistan and was passed down from soldier to soldier in the region.

The witnesses (Ops Team) that were involved with the shooting of the Giant described the Giant as having a thick red beard and long hair of the same color. The witness continued telling the story of his Team going inside the cave and seeing human bones. This led the soldiers to believe this Giant was a cannibal.

One of the Team members was impaled by a weapon the Giant wielded before the Squad could respond. It was a long spear or lance that the Giant swiftly maneuvered to kill the soldier. The whole Squad fired at this giant targeting the head and face, and it took thirty seconds to drop the Giant. According to this one witness, the United States Government didn't disclose the event and has no intention to do so in the future. The witness said that the Government couldn't explain the existence of this Giant because "they don't match with the way we explain our world." (www.theexplan.net/378/The Giant of Kandahar)

It was reported that the Giant weighed eleven hundred pounds, as estimated by the C-130 Cargo plane team that transported the body from the pick-up location to the United States. One of the witnesses remembers that one of the pilots noted a "terrible stench of musk and dirt" exuding from the Giant's cadaver. It smelled like a man "who didn't shower for ten years." (The witness told Marzulli that the odor was more intense than that of a skunk, close to smelling like the pungent stench of a pile of decomposing corpses.)

This giant wore a canvas or animal hide to protect his feet, like a pair of moccasins. There was a search online, and they retrieved the original interview. In this research information, the witness details the encounter with this huge being in a remote area near Kandahar, Afghanistan. Marzulli calls the witness "The Shooter" due to his involvement in the giant's killing. Marzulli claims he had interviewed this witness three times on the phone and at different times. Marzulli never found any discrepancies in his story through all his conversations with the witness. Having seen no change in his account, Marzulli was convinced the event was real. After those meetings with the witness, Marzulli decided to meet the military in person in an undisclosed location.

Marzulli, coincidentally on one of his trips to meet with "The Shooter," found out his driver served in Afghanistan a few years after the giant-killing event. "Mr. D." (the second witness) was interviewed by Marzulli in his documentary series "Watcher X" and said:

When we returned to the base after our routine recon mission, we could hear our fellow soldiers talk about a unit that had found and killed a person inside or at the cave entrance. At first, they did not think much about the stories being bantered. Then they heard them say that the fellow's size was three times that of a human. And that is had more fingers and toes than an ordinary man; that he had red hair and that a particular unit was looking for him...."

In Marzulli's documentary, he shows an iron tip weighing about thirteen pounds. If this tip were placed on a pole to make a spear, it would be difficult for an ordinary man to maneuver it due to its weight and size. A similar iron tip was found in Michigan and given to an Indian Chief of a reservation. "The Shooter" claims to have seen this same iron tip in the hands of the Giant during the Kandahar attack. The same iron tip type that killed his soldier teammate. Archeologists have found Giant bones (skeletons) on the American continent and across the U.S. It would make sense that the Giants made similar spear points throughout their history on Earth and in their travels. Some researchers claim that men dressed in black, saying they worked with the Smithsonian Institute, picked up the giant bones and hauled them back to Washington, DC. Did our government hide these giant artifacts from the public because they also took bones from almost all digging sites? Making the Kandahar Giant something they would hide from the people would make sense if secrecy had been a common routine of our government practices in the past. But why? In American Archeology in 1900, the academic world drew a clear political line of total denial of the existence of such giants. And this policy, for some reason, seems to work these days, as the event in 2002 of the Giant of Kandahar appears they protect the secrecy of the phenomena.

Marzulli's video reenactment shows how the giant leaps onto the clearing, pierces Dan with his weapon, and then holds him in mid-air as the spear goes through the soldier's body. Then the giant advances on the rest of the Special Ops Squad. Without hesitation, they all fire their weapons at the face of the giant, knowing the body shots would not kill him quickly. "Shoot him in the face! Shoot him in the face!" They yell at each other. The Squad had high-powered weapons that each carried, firing simultaneously at the giant's face for thirty seconds, killing him. All these soldiers firing high-powered military weapons at this giant for thirty seconds prove they were up against a huge creature. The soldiers were ordered to lie about this killing of the giant incident. Their superior officers told them to tweak the order of the events. That is why "The Shooter" (witness) took so long to talk about the incident. The Squad was furious over the secrecy, mainly because their team members were killed or injured that day. On the Defense Department press release page, in which all military casualties are listed, there was no report involving a giant. Likewise, there are no reports of an entire patrol disappearing in Afghanistan. Cover up from the upper echelon or even the top of our government – the President? (Snopes.com Bethania Palma)

I know L.A. Marzulli, and he is an honest God-fearing man who is a comprehensive investigator. If he interviewed witnesses in 2016 about the Kandahar Giant, he did it with professionalism. The whistle-blowers Marzulli interviewed were my military brothers, and if they fought a Giant to save their Squad's life, I could believe the incident was truthful. This author does not promote this story as a witness or close my mind to other possibilities which could have happened. My interest in this story was that if this story is one hundred percent accurate, the Giant was a Nephilim, a (fallen angel) offspring of human women and fallen angels, as stated in Genesis in the Bible. In his conclusion, L.A. Marzulli determined that the Giant of Kandahar was a Nephilim giant.

Locations of Giant Skeletons Found – Proof of Nephilim?

Suppose you have seen archeological documents about Egyptian buildings and bass reliefs showing evidence of enormous human beings interacting with smaller men. There were differences between the two human races, as depicted in Egyptian drawings. Most Archeologists would agree that the ancient people saw something; they would draw it as close as possible to their ancient knowledge and perception. So, these artists saw a difference between these two types of humans. The Sumerian giant has six fingers, like the Nephilim and Kandahar Giants. The brain would have had to be larger and more complex to control these extra digits. This would demonstrate that the giants would possess a peculiar intelligence. There have been elongated heads found in Egyptian tombs and giant skeletons that are being hidden from the public by the governments (Egypt and world governments). Again, why all the secrecy by governments? More than likely, secretive groups in control of these governments organize the flow of knowledge to us people of ordinary status. This author believes the control by the elites is not a conspiracy but has been in control of humans for thousands of years (High Priest, Kings, Royal Bloodlines).

North America has a peculiar trait insofar as the prehistoric cultures are concerned, an element called UPT or Unique Physical Type: It is a series of giant humanoid skeletons with a hyper-extended cranium, extra dental structure (double row of teeth) directly inside the tombs or cemeteries of Adeba-Hopewell, archaic cultures and complicated rituals of the South-East. Historians, Antiquarians, and Archeologists have collected data all over the U.S., even though the largest concentration of these UPT remains are in the Ohio River Valley and along the Mississippi River. The written records from these findings are still available within the Municipalities of Counties and Cities. The Smithsonian Institute conducted internal and external investigations on the study of giants. A government-controlled Institute took giant skeletons and bones away for storage away from public view. In May 1841 – in Franklin (Kentucky), several skeletons were dug out from a farm's field and taken away. These stories of bones being taken from people digging up giant remains are not uncommon. Going back to the Kandahar story, it would appear the government has been hiding secrets of his phenomenon for hundreds of years. But why? Are these the remains of the Nephilim that survived and moved worldwide to keep hiding from human civilizations?

Giant Skeletons Found Across the World

In 1924, the New York Times reported, "A huge skeleton, believed to be that of a prehistoric human being, was discovered in Salmon River Country by two members of the State Highway Department, who brought their find to the city.

Largely intact bones – said to be of a woman more than eight feet tall – the bones were found on a cliffside about fifty feet deep, according to a report from Lewiston. The Times continued: "Belief that the person was of an herbivorous race was expressed owing to the peculiar formation of the jaws and teeth. The upper and lower jaws each had only ten teeth, all of which were intact." The Times also said the skeleton was sent to the Smithsonian for study. In my opinion (author), that means the skeleton disappeared from public view going to the Smithsonian.

Another story by the New York Times in 1941 tells of a man's skull found in Chile sixty feet underground during a coal mining operation. "Experts determined the man had been nine to ten feet tall.

There were many findings in Central America of giant skeletons with enormous skulls. Some did not look real, but we have no proof of whether they were authentic skeletons or computer enhanced. The internet is flooded with stories like that about giants living throughout the U.S., as well as elsewhere in the world. "The Nephilim were on the Earth in those ancient days – and also afterward – when the sons of God went into the daughters of humans, who bore children to them." (NIV) Genesis 6, Ezekiel 32, and Numbers 13 are the only passages that mention the Nephilim by that term. (Some Bible versions say "giants" instead of Nephilim.)

In most countries, archeologists have found burial sites with seven to ten feet tall giants with double rows of teeth and reddish hair and beards. These giants had "jaws that could fit over the head of a normal-sized human." Across America, hundreds of burial mounds contain skeletons seven to ten feet tall and have six toes and six fingers. Like humans, they came from different races. Giants were found in West Virginia, New York, New England, Illinois, Minnesota, Wisconsin, and the Ohio basin. All the giants found were similar, with red hair and double rows of teeth and six digits. These giants were smaller than the Kandahar or Biblical Nephilim giants. Could they be a product of genetic changes due to the environment or breeding with normal size humans over time?

Modern-day Archeologists and Anthropology have nearly sealed the door on our imagination, broadly interpreting the North American past as devoid of anything unusual in the way of great cultures and unusual demeanor. The Smithsonian has been saddled with claims that it deliberately destroyed giant bones sent to it from multiple sources, not to give credence to Biblical accounts of Nephilim. Most people think the bones are in a hidden place away from people to see the truth about these giants. Why would the Smithsonian do that and hide giant skeleton bones? Because big ancient humans would challenge the theory of evolution is one theory. It would show we devolved – not evolved. As suggested in this book, our bodies do not compare to the giants in ancient times. For one thing, they supposedly lived longer than normal modern humans. We may open crates at the Smithsonian storage facility and find the missing bones of some giants from long ago. Then they will have to explain why they hide the skeletons of giants. (Syd Albright at silverfix@roadrun ner.com)

"The Smithsonian could have been seen as stupid because they ignored an aspect of their findings that the public sees as intriguing. From a psychological standpoint, they are doing battle with their own shadow. It is a battle that can't be won." (Dr. Gregg Little, AP Magazine)

In the Mediterranean Countries, they have dug up huge giants with elongated skulls like those in the U.S. But most of these finds are much larger skeletons in Greece, Italy, Egypt, and Turkey. Some reach up to twelve feet tall with a double row of teeth and six digits on their feet and hands. Also, the typical red hair and beards are found even in Chinese dig sites. The claim made earlier that the Nephilim exist underground today could be possible as many eyewitnesses have seen them.

My summary of this research

I am open-minded about these Nephilim giants and even the idea that some giants still exist underground and in caves today. Jesus spoke about them and that they were around in Noah's days, as he told his disciples, "There were giants in the land at the time of the great flood." Then Jesus said that the Nephilim would return near the end times again. The Bible speaks of the Nephilim giants in Genesis, making me think that they will return or come up from their underground hiding places to usher at the end of humanity. There is tremendous evidence worldwide that archeologists have dug up giant skeletons proving that they once existed and inhabited most of our Earth. This book does not list modern-day stories of sightings by people of giants. Ancient burial sites that I did not list are abundant with proof of giants, and in most cases, the government and academia hide the truth from us. The Nephilim are fallen angels from long ago, and if they have the supernatural power to come back to Earth, they also prove their capabilities to this author of their ability to return. Will it be an alien false flag? As I mentioned earlier in this book? Now it is possible with the military's disclosure of UAPs and their finally admitting aliens' existence. Since I know L.A. Marzulli, I believe the "Giant of Kandahar" story at face value. Could it have been a very large human Afghan? We will never know the truth, but this attack happened to US soldiers in Afghanistan, where the Nephilim lived in ancient times.

16

SPIRITS, GHOSTS, AND ANGELS

We will try to dissect the differences between spirits: angels, and ghosts and the capacity of each in the language of the Bible.

There are questions about whether (Luke 24:37-43) introduces a Bible contradiction. In this passage, Jesus said that a spirit (as some version states, "a ghost") does not have flesh, bone, or blood as living humans do. After Jesus' resurrection, he met with his disciples and proved that he had flesh and blood by asking them to touch him. Further, Jesus demonstrates his physical presence; he ate boiled fish. But is there a fundamental contradiction? Or are we just looking at a misunderstanding caused by the modern interpretation of the terms used by Jesus? We should look at these critical verses (verses Luke 37 and 39) in the Bible in different English translations.

"But they were startled and frightened and thought they saw a spirit. (Luke 24:37)

"See my hands and feet; that is I, Jesus said." "He said, "Touch me and see." Jesus went on saying, "for a spirit does not have flesh and bones as you see that I have." (Luke 24:39)

The disciples were confused and shocked, thinking they saw a ghost. (Luke 24:37 NIV)

Jesus repeated, "look at my hands and my feet." "It is I!" "Touch me and see; a ghost does not have flesh and bones, as you see I have." (Luke 24:39 NIV) (Troy Lacey – Answers in Genesis)

The Greek word used in (Luke 37:39) is (pneuma), which refers to many different things in the New Testament (NT). These verses it is translated variously as "spirit or ghost." In other parts of the scriptures, it is translated as soul, spirit, a demon (unclean spirit), the divine nature of Christ, human breath, and the wind. In other terminology, it usually refers to an angelic being it is never translated as an angel.

All the instances of an angel(s) mentioned in the NT are from the Greek word (aggelos pronounced ang'-el-os). This could be the likely cause for the alleged contradiction. In (Hebrews 1:7 and 1:14), angels are described as spirits and ministering spirits, respectively.

There are overlapping similarities with the Greek terms that mean about the same as the New Testament but refer to different things. That is, pneuma usually relates to something other than an angel.

In Acts 12:15 in the New Testament, the disciples feared that Peter had been killed in prison when he (unexpectedly) showed up at the door. Rhoda answered the door and told the disciples that Peter was outside the gate; they said to her that "it is his angel" (aggelos). The disciples believed that the soul of a faithful follower of God finally left its body, and the soul became like an angel. Thus, they cannot take a form of a physical form of a human. They could have also believed it was Peter's guardian angel (a concept alluded to by Jesus in (Matthew 18:10).

The alleged contradiction comes into play by taking the Greek words for spirit and angel as equal in all usages when they are different. Some Biblical experts say Jesus made a mistake with his (Luke 24) statement. Some are saying Jesus' words were wrong because they ignored passages about angels being able to take physical form and eat (Genesis 19:3). Or Jesus' words are contradictory if he claimed that ghosts (in the modern sense of disembodied, deceased humans) existed when he said he wasn't a ghost. This was undoubtedly a case of misconstruing the intricacies of Greek words. Yes, an angel may be called a spirit, but it is not to be confused with the word spirit (pneuma) used in the New Testament.

Jesus may have been calming his disciples down about the ghost comment and might have corrected a bit of Jewish folklore. Pneuma can also mean "a human soul that has left the body" (in other words, a disembodied spirit or what modern people today think of as a ghost). Some Jews during that time of Jesus believed that the soul stayed near the dead body for three days just before the human came back to life. After three days, the soul moved on, so it was unlikely the body would return to life. The soul, as the Jewish people thought, would either go to Sheol if it was wicked or was transformed into an angel and went to Abraham's Bosom if it was believing (Luke 16:22-23). The Jewish concept of a ghost or spirit is different from the Western concept of a ghost. They thought the soul stayed around the dead body for three days and then left for its destination, either a bad or good destination. What this passage in the Bible and the Jewish beliefs are saying is that the spirit or ghost leaves the Earth for its reward or penalty and leaving Earth. In a sense saying ghosts or spirits don't hang around on Earth. There are cases in the time of Jesus where people might have been in a coma and temporarily dead as they witnessed it. The person would return to life or come out of the coma in a short time, giving credence to the three-day waiting of the soul to leave the body. Or be a self-resurrected body brought to life after the coma. Elijah and Elisha performed miracles through the power of God to bring people back to life. Today, with modern medicine and technology, we can ascertain more certainty than we used to be of pronouncing someone legally dead. Even a hundred years ago, the ability to officially pronounce someone dead was much harder to determine. (Troy Lacey – Answers in Genesis)

Ghosts are the most misunderstood of all spiritual creatures and the most misrepresented in literature and film. The word "ghost" means spirit or soul. The use of the term (Holy Ghost as a synonym for the Holy Spirit). "Souls belong only to human beings." It has been written that humans are the only beings who have both a spiritual nature (a soul) and a physical body. Angels and demons can present themselves to us physically; the bodies they adopt are not part of their nature. People have recently seen their pets in a ghost or spirit form in their presence and even heard them. Does that mean they have souls or spirits? Some have captured their pets on film inside their homes. Can this mean that with modern technology (cameras), people see animals have spirits? In my opinion, everything with a life force (energy) can have a spirit. (This Author's opinion)

A disembodied soul is a ghost, in other words, a soul that has separated from the physical body when death occurs to that physical body. The Church teaches us that, after death, each of us will be judged by God. As a result of that judgment, we will go to Heaven or hell. However, the ones that go to Heaven will spend some time in Purgatory, being cleansed of their sins. Cleansing their sins makes them pure so they can enter God's presence. As I was researching this "Heaven and hell" explanation, I had to question where the sinners will end up "straight to hell," as the old saying states. No Purgatory for sinners? I was always taught that some people get stuck in Purgatory (the midway point to Heaven) upon dying. Our modern-day ghost hunters say that ghosts (spirits) are lost souls that can't find their way to the light of Heaven. I don't think they are lost souls. It is more residual energy from the human spirit since we all have energy in our bodies. Traditionally, ghosts have been seen as those souls in Purgatory. These ghosts are in Purgatory because they have "unfinished business" in the sense of atonement for sins.

Unlike angels and demons, ghosts are tied to a particular place and maintain a presence until they leave Earth after they finish their unfinished business. Those places you find ghosts have something to do with the sins they must still atone for. Saints in Heaven occasionally appear to us here on Earth, but when they do, we see them in their glory. As Christ, Himself told us in the rich man and Lazarus parable, souls in hell cannot appear to the living. Did Christ mean that there are no evil spirits that lurk around the living? Then, what we have seen in popular culture is that evil spirits attacking people and putting fear in them are all wrong – they are not from Hell and not evil.

So, ghosts are good? Not evil? Contrary to many portrayals in literature and film, ghosts are never malevolent creatures. How could we read into this evil ghost theory in a very wrong way? This would make these ghosts we run into non-threatening but scare people by passing through their location of atonement. They are souls on their way to Heaven by way of Purgatory. When souls fully atone for their sins and enter Heaven, they will be saints. By what Christ said in the New Testament, these ghosts or spirits are incapable of misleading or harming those of us still here on Earth. "Evil spirits cannot appear before people that are still living."

What are Poltergeists?

These spirits have been referred to as trouble-making ghosts because of their physical actions to make noise and move objects. What are these malevolent spirits that look like ghosts in films and TV shows? Let's set aside the fact that we should not be taking our theology from pop culture (instead, it should take its theology from the Church); we might; call those spirits poltergeists. The problem is when we try to define what a poltergeist is. The word poltergeist is a German term that means a "noisy ghost"- that is, a ghost that moves things to disrupt the lives of humans. The poltergeist causes disturbances and loud noises, as reported by people. And may even cause harm to human beings, but not many of those cases were directly caused by the poltergeist itself. It might be that people running from the noise in fear got hurt by their accidents. (The Differences Between Angels, Demons, and Ghosts)

17

FAIRIES AND CRYPTIDS

There are no single origins of stories and myths about fairies but a collection of folk beliefs from disparate sources. Theories about the origins of fairies include casting them as either demoted angels or demons in the Christian tradition, as minor deities in Pagan systems, as spirits of the dead, as prehistoric precursors to humans, or as elementals. A fairy is often described as a magical creature with a human appearance, small stature, and supernatural powers with a penchant for trickery. At other times it has been used to describe any magical creature, such as goblins and gnomes. The name fairy has been used as an adjective, with a meaning equal to "enchanted" or "magical."

Legends of fairies in how to protect yourself from their magical powers. It is said that people used protective charms like; church bells, wearing clothing inside out, four-leaf clover, and food. Fairies were said to haunt specific locations and lead travelers in the wrong direction using will-o-the-wisps. Before modern medicine, fairies were often blamed for making people sick, particularly with tuberculosis and birth deformities.

In the folklore of Ireland, the mythic aes sidhe, or "little folk," have come to a modern meaning somewhat inclusive of fairies. The Celtic Revival also saw fairies established as a canonical part of Celtic cultural heritage. The Scandinavian elves also served as an influence. Folklorists have depicted fairies as unworthy dead, the children of Eve, a kind of demon, a species independent of humans, an older race of humans, and fallen angels. The folklorist or mythological elements combine Celtic, Germanic, and Greco-Roman elements. Fairies emerged from various earlier beliefs, which lost currency with the advent of Christianity. All these disparate explanations are not necessarily incompatible, and fairies may be traced to multiple sources.

Christian mythology, King James, in his dissertation Daemonologie, stated that the term "fairies" referred to illusory spirits (demonic entities) that prophesied to, consorted with, and transported individuals they served. In medieval times, a witch or sorcerer who had a pact with a familiar spirit might receive these services.

Demoted Angels

The early Christians held that fairies were a class of "demoted" angels. One story described a group of angels revolting, and God ordered the gates of Heaven shut: those still in Heaven remained angels, those left in hell became demons, and all caught in between became fairies. Some angels, not being Godly enough, yet not evil enough for hell, was thrown out of Heaven. The tradition of paying a "teind" or tithe to hell; as fallen angels, although not quite devils, they could be viewed as subjects of Satan.

The Theosophist circles in England of the nineteenth century believed in the "angelic" nature of fairies which was reported. Entities referred to as Devas were said to guide many processes of nature, such as the evolution of organisms and the growth of plants. Many fairies (Devas) resided inside the Sun (Solar Angels). Earthbound Devas included nature spirits, elementals, and fairies, which were described as appearing as forms of colored flames, roughly the size of a human.

In modern times, even in recent years, people have seen fairies in the forest of Scotland and England. Some witnesses have even taken videos and pictures of them. They looked like tiny humans about ten inches tall, wearing clothing and hats resembling humans but much smaller beings. People have seen flying fairies that looked like dragonflies but had human-shaped bodies with transparent wings. These fairies seemed smaller than the other ten inches tall fairies walking on the ground and were only three inches long with larger wing spans of over three inches. Of course, there are computer graphic images that could make these fairy sightings look real, making them a sophisticated myth more believable than mere words of years past. This author believes that these fairies and supernatural entities could be angels that take on a different form as angels can do, being supernatural shapeshifters according to their mission from God. We could go further and say the fairies could be dimensional and come and go in our environment at will. The invisibility of these tiny entities is a possibility that we must consider also. Nobody has ever captured a fairy or found a dead fairy from all indications throughout history. (Fairies/Cryptid Wiki/Fandom)

Cryptids, Monsters, and other Mysteries

It might seem strange for this chapter to be in an angel book or a Catholic Exchange discussing cryptids. Let me paraphrase Tertullian's retort: What have cryptids to do with Christ? The proven existence or non-existence of Bigfoot, Nessie, Sea Serpents, and their ilk has nothing to do with the saints, the Eucharist, the dogmas of the faith, or the existence of God. Well, these cryptid stories may not directly connect these strange animals to the faithful's beliefs, but there might still be some kernel of a connection. Our faith does not depend on whether these creatures exist, but we can still use them as springboards for discussion for some surprisingly deep philosophical and theological reflections. We need not rely on fuzzy photos, out-of-focus videos, or suspect footprints to stake our theological claims or hold philosophical conversations.

In clarifying terms, Cryptozoology refers to studying and hunting for hidden, unclassified animals. This also involves looking for and studying mysterious creatures like Bigfoot, the Loch Ness Monster, and extinct animals. There are reports of people seeing (living dinosaurs or surviving Tasmanian tigers). These such names creatures are deemed "cryptids."

Cryptozoology is not a recognized branch of mainstream science, and many cryptozoologists find themselves on the bitter end of skeptics' derisive comments. This, however, has not stopped the popularity of the studies, books, TV shows, and movies that all reflect our love for these monsters and other creatures. Such popular presentations do little to lend cryptozoology more credibility; monsters, it seems, remain the realm of intellectual immaturity, and young people like the scary stories these creatures are used for.

Cryptozoology is not a standard realm for theological discourse, though there are exceptions. We must visit the Bible to find these exceptions to how these cryptids relate to the theological discourse. If we look at the strange creatures in Bible Scripture, such as the Leviathan and the Behemoth (Job 40-41), or the Dragon in (Daniel 14:23-27), through a lens of cryptozoology, we might see where these creatures relate to the Biblical events. Biblical scholars who adhere to a literalistic interpretation of Scripture would claim that it is proof that dinosaurs survived into recent times. And that Earth could not be as old as geologists seem to indicate. Recent studies suggest that the world is older than these Religious Scholars claim. They also claim that humankind is much older than five thousand years of existence. But it still does not preclude that these cryptids are still on the Earth today, hiding from us in remote places or deep under the seas. Cryptozoologists and Theologians differ in these studies about when these creatures existed on Earth. As I said, these creatures still exist in limited numbers surviving the thousands of years hiding from humans.

In his podcast "Jimmy Akin's Mysterious World," Jimmy Akin discussed Bigfoot's mystery. As with other cryptid topics he discusses on his podcast. Akin and his co-host Dom Bettinelli examine "claims and counter-claims." They discuss the possibility of the existence of Bigfoot and what effect it would have on the faith perspective of people. In their discussion, they address some of the issues connected to Christianity if it turns out Bigfoot was real. Would this Bigfoot represent the missing link, or would Bigfoot be a relative of the Nephilim? So, there would be some tangential connection between cryptozoology and Christianity.

Evangelists and apologists have used stories of interest in the "popular culture" of their audience since St. Paul referenced works and ideas of Greco-Roman culture in his epistles and his preaching. In St. Paul's speech to the philosophers in Athens (17:16-34). Today, we can use stories of Sasquatch. Ogopogo, and the Ropen as a spark to deeper discussions of God and his plan for us. (Cryptids, Monsters, and the Mysteries of our Faith)

Biblical Monsters are also Mentioned

Sea Monsters:

Most Biblical authors were not seafarers, and the Bible still has several references to various sea monsters, most notably Jonah's giant fish (Jonah 1:17) and the infamous Leviathan (Psalms 74:14). Famous seafaring Greeks had plenty of myths about monsters that swam up from the deeps to devour ships and sailors. Could these seafaring Greeks' imaginations run wild over finding ancient fossils, which could explain the myths?

Gorgons:

Speaking of seafaring Greeks, it is known that the Greeks were trading with the southern Levantine coastal city of Tel Dor as early as the sixth century B.C.E. Along with selling goods and supplies, the Greeks also traded myths about Gorgons. The tale implies that Gorgons can turn people into stone with a single look. While archeologists dug sites in Tel Dor, they uncovered a mask depicting one of these Gorgons. Has there been evidence of these Gorgons excavated at Tel Dor? In every story or myth, there is an element of truth within that story.

Beelzebul:

I can't end this list of monsters without mentioning the prince of demons himself, Beelzebul. Beelzebul is frequently associated with Satan; this equivalence is never explicit in the Bible. Beelzebul is better understood as a play on the name of one of Yahweh's chief rivals, the Canaanite god Baal. This idea in the play on Baal's name can be found in (Kings 1:18) where Baal is mocked with the name Baalzebub or "the lord of the flies." He was also called the god of fertility. Jesus calls Satan Beelzebub (Matthew 12:27). It was written that Jehu destroyed Baal in Israel around the ninth and eighth centuries BCE. In Syria, a Temple built for Baal called the Temple Palmyra still exists today. (Biblical Monsters – Biblical Archeology Society)

Baal, the god worshipped in many ancient Middle Eastern communities, especially among Canaanites, was considered Baal a fertility deity and one of the most important gods in the pantheon. A Semitic common noun Baal (Hebrew ba al) meant "owner" or "lord," in more general use; for example, a Baal of wings was a winged creature, and, in the plural, Baalim of arrows indicated archers. In that capacity, Baal was considered a prince of fertility and, in that title, "Lord of the Earth."

Ugaritic texts tell of other fertility aspects of Baal, such as his relations with Anath, his consort and sister, and his siring a divine bull calf from a heifer. All this was part of Baal's fertility role, which, when fulfilled, meant an abundance of crops and fertility for animals and humans. Dagan was the father of Baal, and he invented the plow for farming grain. He was also the god of vegetation. His cult was attested as early as twenty-five hundred BC according to texts found at Ras Shamra; Dagan was second in importance only to El (God Himself). In Palestine, where he was mainly a god of the Philistines where he had several sanctuaries, including those at Beth-Dagan in Asher (Joshua 19:27), Gaza (Judges 16-23), and Ashdod (1 Samual 5:2-7). It seems the father Dagan and the son Baal were knowledgeable people ahead of their time. Were they of a supernatural nature? These leaders in ancient times possessed intelligence and power that could be considered strange or otherworldly. (Dagan/Semitic god/Britannica)

18

THE SHAPESHIFTERS

"You are from your father, the devil, and you choose to do your father's desires. He was a murderer from the beginning and did not stand by the truth because there was no truth in him. He speaks according to his nature when he lies, for he is a liar and the father of lies." (John 8:44) A confusing Bible quote, to be for sure. We will get more into what this Bible verse means.

In the literature of all cultures, a fascinating character emerges called the "Shapeshifter." Such characters are not what they say they are and appear differently when they need to be different. Mostly these Shapeshifters try to appear friendly and virtuous to fool people, proving to be deceptive. The Bible cautions us not to believe these deceptive individuals, and "there are false prophets who come in my name, says the Lord." One of the first examples of a Shapeshifter in the Bible is written in Genesis, the Garden of Eden, with the serpent appearing before Eve and persuading her to eat from the apple of wisdom. This serpent was deceptive and lied to Eve about the outcome of how the knowledge would change Adam and Eve's lives forever and even human destinies. Cain is the first brother who turns into a murderer, and he is deceived by the false wisdom the serpent gave to him through his family lineage. Rebekah deceives her husband and eldest son to get the family blessing for Jacob. Deceit appears chromosomal in that family, as both Jacob and his uncle Laban are not above false promises. This means that "Shapeshifting" comes not only in bodily appearances but in lies and deceit, like in these early Biblical events.

The psychological reality is that Shapeshifting isn't just "out there" but also "in here": we all have various impulses fighting within us, allowing versions of ourselves to appear at different times. A name for a more significant aspect of our darker selves we don't want to talk about is our "Shadow." The biblical injunctions to confess, repent, transform, or convert are all calls to acknowledge that our characters are ever being formed, and the shape of our actions is constantly shifting. The power of the Holy Spirit, God in us, is the only force strong enough to turn us from the shadows. (Charismatic Characters: The Shapeshifter)

In the New Testament, Pharisees appear to be morally virtuous defenders of the law but are revealed to be more interested in locking God in a box of rituals. Judas is the archetype of shifting priorities, betraying Jesus with a kiss on the cheek. Satan, the father of lies, is the most important Shapeshifter in the New Testament. By Jesus' time, Satan is known as the Devil, the personification of evil. The Devil tempted Jesus with power, possessions, and pride if Jesus would only bow to him. That is how a Shapeshifter will appeal to our lower desires to subvert our higher goals. The other name for Satan is Lucifer, "bearer of light," which describes the deep deception of evil wrapped in a shiny package and filled with lies wrapped in half-truths. The book of Revelations reveals Satan as the devil, the leader of all evil forces that tries to pull us from God. The Christian tradition has identified the first betrayer, the Serpent, as the real Satan Himself. The ultimate victory is God's, but the battles are fierce, and the price is steep: God was sacrificed on the cross – Jesus Christ.

I will list a few Bible verses mentioning Shapeshifting:

> *After these things, he appeared in another form to two of them as they walked into the country.*

> — MARK 16:12 ESV

*The coming of the lawless one is by the activity of Satan
with all power and false signs and wonders.*

— 2 THESSALONIANS 2:9 ESV

*And a great sign appeared in Heaven: a woman clothed
with the sun, with the moon under her feet. On her
head was a crown of twelve stars. She was pregnant
and crying out in the pain and agony of giving birth.
Another sign appeared in Heaven: behold, a great red
dragon, with seven heads and ten horns, and on his
heads seven diadems. She gave birth to a male child,
one who is to rule all nations with a rod of iron, but her
child was caught up to God and his throne.*

— REVELATION 12:1-17 ESV

*And I saw a beast rising out of the sea, with ten horns and
seven heads, with ten diadems on its horns and blasphe-
mous names on its heads. The beast I saw was like a
leopard; its feet were like bears, and its mouth was like a
lion's. One of its heads seemed to have a mortal wound,
but its mortal wound was healed, and the whole Earth
marveled as they followed the beast. (What does the
Bible Say About Shapeshifting?)*

— REVELATION 13:1-18 ESV

Egyptian Text Describes Jesus Changing His Shape

A newly translated, 1,200-year-old religious text written in the Coptic language tells (the story of Jesus' crucifixion) in a way that departs significantly from Biblical accounts. The text was originally from an Egyptian monastery that seems to have ceased operating in the tenth century AD. The manuscript resurfaced in 1910 and was purchased by New York financier J.P. Morgan. Utrecht University historian Roelof van den Broek, who translated the text, says it was written in the name of St. Cyril of Jerusalem, a fourth-century saint. This manuscript was amongst other apocryphal claims; the text says that Jesus had dinner with Pontius Pilate before the crucifixion and that Judas used a kiss on the cheek to identify Jesus. And that those who came to arrest Jesus were told Judas would kiss the real Jesus Christ because Jesus constantly changed his shape. Van de Broek says the fifth century AD canonized the Bible. The apocryphal stories remained popular among Christians long after that. This manuscript is still on display at the (Morgan Library & Museum) in New York City. (Archaeology Magazine)

Can Jesus Shapeshift?

The Egyptian text I just wrote about Jesus being a Shapeshifter and the following story of Jesus as a Shapeshifter is not this author's researched opinion. It is other researchers' theories and findings. These theories are not fully proven or directly printed in the Bible, as we know in the New Testament. The Coptic Books were not included in the Bible, so the truth is mysterious. You, the reader, make your determination as you read this story about Jesus.

According to the Egyptian text's findings, (yes, Jesus can Shape-shift and perform many other miracles. It was when people started to follow Jesus and stopped giving Tithes or financial Donations to the Temple that the Chief Priests of the Jews became angry with Him). Have you wondered why Jesus did not use His miracles to escape his Crucifixion? Since the Bible was compiled or canonized by a group of priests a few hundred years after the Crucifixion of Jesus Christ, certain important information was accidentally or intentionally removed from the New Testament Bible. This information was recorded in "Pseudo-Cyril of Jerusalem on the Life and Passion of Christ – Coptic Apocryphon" by Roelof van den Broek.

Shapeshifting is one of the many miracles Jesus Christ could perform. According to the text, when the Jews asked Judas to deliver Jesus Christ, they asked Judas: "How shall we arrest the right person, for Jesus does not have a single shape, but Jesus's appearances change. Sometimes he is ruddy; sometimes he is white, sometimes Jesus is red, sometimes he is wheat-colored, sometimes Jesus is pallid like ascetics, sometimes looks youthful; sometimes an older man; other times Jesus' hair is stringy and black, sometimes his hair is curly, sometimes appears tall, sometimes Jesus seems short. In simple words, we have never seen Jesus in the same appearance." It is for this reason; that Judas told the Jews that since he will appear differently, I will give you a sign which I shall give to those who will follow me: He whom I shall kiss on his mouth and embrace and to whom I shall say: 'Hail rabbi,' he is your man. Arrest Him!"

Pilate tried multiple times to prevent Jesus Christ from being Crucified and even offered his only son to be killed in Jesus Christ's place. Jesus performed another miracle by becoming incorporeal ("not composed of matter, having no material existence, "ghostly presences"). When Jesus was brought to Pilate, Pilate described Jesus as having an appearance that was "frightening like (that of) a royal son. Pilate did not know what to do with Jesus, so he sent him to Herod in Galilee, where Jesus Christ came from, so Jesus could not be "unfairly judged in a foreign country." Herod was sent a papyrus written statement from Pilate saying to have "no patience" with Jesus Christ "for one" hour except to put him upon a wooden cross, with his face turned to the sun. Based on the law back then, Pilate could release a prisoner from the prison he selected on every feast. Pilate, at first, wanted to release Jesus and have Barabbas crucified, but the Chief Priests persuaded the crowd to say that they wanted to release Barabbas and Crucify Jesus.

Pilate kept trying, stating to Jesus Christ, "Truly, I want to release you, but I do not know what to do with this rebellious crowd that wants to kill you." Jesus Christ replied, "My Kingdom is not of this world." Pilate offered, "when morning comes, and they accuse me because of you, I shall give them my only son for Crucifixion so they can kill him instead of you." Jesus rejected the offer kindly and requested to proceed with the Crucifixion. Pilate offered to kill his only son the next day instead of killing Jesus again before the Crucifixion. Pilate was so stressed that he fainted, and Jesus helped him back to his feet. Jesus said to him: 'Have you understood that if I wish, I can escape?' Pilate said: 'Yes, my Lord.'"

Have you wondered why the Chief Priests hated Jesus Christ so much? It was all about the money they were not getting in their Temple Tithes from the people. Financial donations were dwindling, with Jesus preaching about the High Priests taking their money and becoming rich off the poor. Jesus told the people that the money being donated was going to the Priests getting rich and not sharing their money with the poor. People shared their livestock, grains, labor, and land with the Priests in the Temple, only to make the Temple corrupt with money changers becoming richer with their Tithes.

Jesus was not only gifted with Supernatural abilities. He also healed people in front of large gatherings of people, which made the towns-people believe Jesus was the Son of Man who was of God. Jesus brought people back to life after being dead, he made the blind see, and he expelled demons from possessed people. The "great multitudes followed him because of the signs he did in healing." After people saw the miracles Jesus performed, they stopped giving Tithes to the Temple Priests, and that enraged the Priests even more. Jesus' popularity grew more significant than their Temple crowds, and Jesus threatened not only money but the Priests' egos because his followers were greater. And everybody that believed in Jesus stopped going to the Jewish Synagogues because they saw the Lord's work with their own eyes. Just like we said today: It is all about the money. Jesus also said that money was "the root of all evil."

Jesus Christ's Shapeshifting (Transfiguration and Metamorphosis) in the Gospels, the New Testament of the Bible

The following verses in the Gospels describe Jesus Christ's shapeshifting using transfiguration. Mark 9:2-3 writes, "After six days, Jesus took Peter, James, and John with him, and led them up a high mountain apart, by themselves. And he metamorphosed before them, and his clothes became dazzling white, like no fuller on Earth could bleach them."

Matthew 17:1-2 writes that Jesus took Peter, James, and his brother John and led them to the top of a mountain by themselves. And metamorphosed before them, Jesus' face shone like the sun in a brilliant bright white light.

Luke 9-29 writes, "And while Jesus was praying, the appearance on his face changed, and his clothes became dazzling white."

Luke 4:29-30 describes that Jesus made a miraculous escape, "They got up, drove him out of town, and led Jesus to the brow of a hill on which their town was built so that they might hurl Jesus off the cliff. But Jesus passed through their midst and went on his way."

Reading these Shapeshifting stories about Jesus would make you more intrigued with Jesus' supernatural powers and make you believe that he was indeed the Son of God. When Jesus talks of being "not of this world" and "money is the root of all evil," his spiritual abilities and closeness to God become much more straightforward. You can say that Jesus, Angels, and the invisible forces all around us in spirit are all extraterrestrial – not from here on Earth. (Christ is a Shapeshifter According to Ancient Egyptian Texts) (Thiaoouba Prophecy)

Shapeshifting in Native American Culture

When people hear the word "shapeshifter," they think of supernatural figures like witches and werewolves. The spiritual practice of shapeshifting travels well beyond a mythical and supernatural scope like the Divine Spiritual powers demonstrated in the Bible.

What is shapeshifting?

A non-Native study of shapeshifting posits that medicine people and shamans used the practice to transform into a part animal to cause harm and destruction rather than good by shooting pieces of bone into their victims, much like a witch would. These shamans were the leaders of their tribes, and their visions were brought about by tobacco laced with other narcotic drugs like psychoactive alkaloids, mescaline, and Peyote from a cactus plant. When these shamans go into their rituals and smoke these drugs, they enter another world, maybe a dimensional one. They would see visions and tell their people what they saw in the future. They tell stories of traveling to these other worlds as animals of their choosing, like bears, coyotes, wolves, mountain lions, and the eagle. The shamans' shapeshifting was more about visualizing these animals, not necessarily being that animal in its natural form.

Tribes such as the Navajo, however, talk about more positive roles of shapeshifting in forming Native American culture. Native American Indians often refer to the practice as "skinwalking." These shapeshifters transform into bears, wolves, and eagles' bodies for healing and protecting their communities. The word Skinwalker puts fear in most Native Americans that know the phenomena firsthand. There are scary stories of Skinwalkers being evil and killing people in and around the Native American reservations. Witnesses have said they appear as an upright huge dog or wolf-like creature with a human shape but are hairy and terrifying. Cryptid researchers cannot trace their origins and don't know if the shamans (some supernatural shamans) are shapeshifting into Skinwalkers to kill people. Is there a sinister side to some shamans? Or do these animals exist as real cryptids, and are the shamans not responsible for these demonic creatures? (Shapeshifting in Native American Culture/Kachina House's Blog)

When does Shapeshifting occur?

Shapeshifting trains our egos to let go and become shapeless so that we can take on the qualities of our chosen animal. This is like most people's meditation to transcend their minds into higher dimensions and consciousness and relax. Getting themselves into this state of consciousness, the Native American Indians used tobacco with

Peyote and other stimulants to induce their dream-like state. This was mostly done during Native American songs, dances, war ceremonies, and hunting rituals, and it takes excellent nimbleness. Native Americans don't use drugs to induce these ceremonies frequently. Mostly they are more benign with tobacco smoke used instead of drugs. By no means is this author saying Native Americans use drugs more than the general population. They don't! Some shamans partake in this hallucinatory practice to increase their otherworldly adventures into a mystic dimension for reading the future and seeking knowledge for their people.

The most common form of shapeshifting happens through dance. The dancers dress in feathers and animal pelts to activate the divine animal spirit in their movements. Instead of moving as the eagle would, the dancer will propel himself in short bursts of momentum and hurl their arms in controlled, swinging movements. This action of the ritualistic dancer doing these reenactments of animals engages their core, mind, and heart in an out-of-body experience where physical human limits presented by the everyday world do not exist. We can see this in any music and dancing event where people work themselves into a frenzied out-of-body state of higher consciousness. The person dancing will get their bodily adrenaline and endorphins at a higher elevation than normal, giving them the feeling of ecstasy.

In hunting, the shapeshifter is associated with cunning, courage, loyalty, and strength. They are central figures in Zunis and Shoshone mythology and clan animals for tribes like the Cherokee and Chippewa. The wolf and Native Americans were closely linked during the time of the early settlers, so much so that they would often kill Native Americans the same way they would a wolf. Our early settlers were not kind to the Native American people, and it was a dark time during the Indian wars with the settlers and their armies. These settlers looked at Indians as savages and treated them like wild animals. A terrible history was produced by the white settlers in their horrific treatment of the American Indians. It was not a wonder that the Indians behaved like wolves to navigate around the settlers to be tough like wolves and survive. The Indians learned the ways of a wolf to improve their survival techniques and outwit their enemies. Again, this falls into the category of shapeshifting to act like a wolf and think like a wolf. But this was more of an adapting to animal characteristics instead of appearing like a real wolf. People who can correctly shapeshift come in touch with their instincts. They can appreciate the spirit of their ancestors and the spirit of living things. (Shapeshifting in Native American Culture/Kachina House's Blog)

A lot of what has been talked about shapeshifting is just the benign practices that are ceremonious for the Native American Indians. But what about the real (Skinwalker creature)? The ones that we see on television and in the movies are terrifying to look at. These creatures, as earlier mentioned, have the potential to kill people and put fear into the Native American people. The police departments get emergency calls often about people seeing strange creatures standing upright like humans, but they look like wolves and mad dogs, as witnesses claim. Native Americans often go missing in the Western United States, believing these missing people are victims of the Skinwalker creature. I had a chance to speak to some of the Hopi Indians in New Mexico. I talked to an older Native American woman about Skinwalkers. She looked at me in fear and walked away in a hurry. I met this young Indian artist right after the elder woman incident. He told me not to talk to older Indians about the Skinwalker experiences they may have had. This young man said that the younger people don't have the same fear of the Skinwalker subject as the older generation. He said that the younger people don't have the cultural teachings the more senior people have had with the stories being handed down from one generation to another.

19

EXTRATERRESTRIALS AND ANGELS

Are aliens in the Bible?

W e need to get on the same page to start talking about aliens and understand the differences in Biblical references.

A true definition of an alien is "anything that belongs to a foreign territory." A person or being who is not a citizen of a country they reside in would be considered an "alien." In the plant and animal world, alien species in a region are often called "invasive species." If we speak about aliens to Earth, it could refer to any being that is not from Earth. Angels and demons that interact with our world could be included in that group. Biblical scriptures indicate these beings and their existence. If you want to call angels and demons "aliens" because they are not originally from Earth, then yes, there are aliens in the Bible. If you are reading this book, especially this Chapter, you are wondering if the Bible teaches anything about life on other planets. Suppose our working definition of aliens will not include angels or demons since they are spiritual beings, not organisms. Any extraterrestrial lifeform foreign to Earth is considered alien to humans. The Bible has nothing to say about the possibility of other life forms other than spiritual in nature and not biological. Any potential for organisms to exist somewhere else besides planet Earth, the Bible makes no references to life in the universe. What we know is that God created the Heavens and the Earth. God created the entire universe. Jesus came to Earth to save sinful humanity. (What does the Bible Say About Aliens? – 2/42 Community Church)

Are Aliens Demons?

Given that the definition of "alien" refers to any foreign being, which leaves room for the term being used to describe a demonic being in scripture, demonic beings are spiritual beings. This means they are part of the spiritual realm, not from another planet. The spiritual realm interacts with the world throughout the Biblical Scriptures. Ephesians 6:12 talks about an enemy not of flesh and blood, including: "rulers, authorities, powers, and forces of evil in Heavenly realms.

2 Corinthians 10:4-5 is written in scripture about fighting a spiritual enemy with "weapons not of this world."

Matthew, chapter 4, the "tempter" meets Jesus in the wilderness.

Genesis 18: Abraham encounters three strangers that do not realize they are angels.

In Matthew and Luke's gospel accounts, Zachariah, Mary, and Joseph all have encounters with angels.

Luke 2: a "host" of angels engage with a group of shepherds.

In most cases, angels and demons are spiritual entities that can be good or bad, depending on if God or Satan commands them. In most Biblical references to demons, people are "possessed" or "filled with" a demonic spirit. So, could someone have a demonic experience and determine that it was an alien? Yes. The further we get into this study of aliens and angels we will get different perspectives of their differences.

Are Angels Aliens?

As with the demons, angels are foreign beings to Earth, so the term "alien" can be used to describe angels. As mentioned earlier in this book, many angels appear like humans and take a bodily form that the person they visit will recognize as humanoid. Angels take human shape not to scare humans with a supernatural appearance. Angels will interact with humans long enough to complete their mission and not stay on Earth for long periods. In the angel's process of shapeshifting to human forms or other animal forms, they can be mistaken for extraterrestrial beings and be mistaken for human beings, as the writer of Hebrews wrote in the Scriptures. "Do not forget to show hospitality to strangers, for by doing, some people have shown hospitality to angels without knowing it." (Hebrews 13-2) In my experiences with the supernatural, if you fear, the entities may be evil – demons. But if it is a very pleasant spiritual feeling, it is divine supernatural energy. Most of my encounters have been a positive, exuberant spiritual stirring feeling. The supernatural entities and angels could be confusing because they all come through some dimensional portal and appear in different forms. (What Does the Bible Say About Aliens? 2/42 Community Church)

In the Judeo-Christian and Islamic traditions, angels have played a huge role in developing these religions. Angels helped create the first human beings, and they revealed sacred scriptures and helped human beings understand religion. Angels procreated with women (Nephilim – Fallen Angels) and helped produce offspring for humans. They were said to transport prophets and seers like; Muhammad or Enoch through the Heavens to receive secret wisdom.

These same angels become warriors in the apocalypse, battling demons and helping to create a new Earth. Since 1947 (Roswell incident), a new extra-terrestrial power has appeared in literature, film, comics, and religious scripture: the alien. Abductees, artists, and religious visionaries claim that aliens (ETs) perform the same actions historically attributed to angels. Aliens today found religions and transported humans to distant worlds, conducting genetic experiments and, in films like "Independence Day," attempting to destroy human civilization. As an experiencer of ETs and angels and their similarities, it has been my question: How do I make sense of these uncanny parallels? In figuring out the angel and extra-terrestrial differences, it is best to use the tools of comparative religions to understand the puzzling parallels between angels and aliens. When either angel or an extra-terrestrial visits you, you are seemingly in another world, almost like a dream world state where your mind is being controlled. Angels seem to telepathically deliver a message or warning or talk in a human voice conversation. The Bible states that angels will speak to humans with their messaging if they take on a human form, which is why you don't know if they are human or angels. Extra-terrestrials usually come in their alien form to upload or download consciousness memories or take DNA samples. When they sedate you with magnetic energy, it leaves you with very little memory of the event. Unlike angel visits, the extra-terrestrials leave you with fear and confusion, whereas angels leave pleasant spiritual energy you vibrate from. (Angels and Aliens; M. Dillon – Humanities Core)

What would the existence of aliens mean to Christianity?

If scientists or the Government proved the existence of alien life in the universe, it would not negate any of the Scripture. There are no conflicts in the Bible with the potential for life outside the Earth, as in extra-terrestrials. Scripture claims that God created the Heavens and the Earth and made all people in the image of God. Jesus is the only way to salvation, and the only way to Heaven is through him. The Bible is a witness to Jesus' salvation powers and Jesus' God-given right to decide peoples' destinies to Heaven or hell. It is said that all these statements will be factual even if extraterrestrials are proven to exist. So, there is no change in thinking regarding the total disclosure of ETs and the Bible's interpretation.

Humans were created with the ability to wonder about worldly and otherworldly life forms that may exist. The basic premise is that "we can't be alone in this giant universe." Our imaginations cause us to explore and ponder the depths of God and his creations. When we look at the stars at night, we see God's majesty and awe on display and feel we are not alone in this universe. Exploring our universe opens us up to a whole new picture of how great our God is. While exploring other planets, we find intelligent life forms other than Earth that will not diminish anything in scripture. We will accept that God created all life, and we will know they are part of the same creation miracles of God as we are. If we follow Jesus, we are "not of this world" anyway. We are called to Heaven, which is technically a different place than Earth, making us extra-terrestrial.

The Bible and Aliens Mentioned in Scripture

Hebrews 11:3, "By faith, we understand that the universe was created by the words of God so that what is seen was not made out of things that are visible."

Psalm 19:1, "To the choirmaster. A Psalm of David. The Heavens declare the glory of God, and the sky above proclaims his handiwork."

Psalm 8:3-4, "When I look at your Heavens, the work of your fingers, the moon, and the stars, which you have set in place, what is the man that you are mindful of him, and the son of man that you care for him?"

John 1:3, "All things were made through God, and without Him was not anything made that was made." (What Does the Bible Say About Aliens? – 2/42 Community Church)

Ezekiel 1:1-28, Now it came to pass in the thirtieth year, in the fourth month, in the fifth day of the month, as I was among captives by the river of Chebar, that the Heavens were opened, and I saw visions of God.

Ezekiel 1:4, And I looked, and behold, a whirlwind came out of the north, a great cloud, and a fire enfolding itself, and a brightness was about it, and out of the midst thereof as the color of amber, out of the midst of the fire.

Isaiah 13:5, They come from a far country, from the end of Heaven, even the Lord, and the weapons of his indignation, to destroy the whole land.

Revelation 9:7-11, And the shapes of the locusts were like unto horses prepared unto battle, and on their heads were crowns like gold, and their faces were as the faces of men.

Isaiah 45:12, I have made the Earth, and created man upon it: I, even my hands, have stretched out the Heavens, and all their host I have commanded.

Ezekiel 1:7, And their feet were straight, and the sole of their feet was like the sole of a calf's foot: they sparkled like the color of burnished brass.

Hebrews 11:13, These all died in faith, not having received the promises, but having seen them afar off, and were persuaded of them, embraced them, and confessed that they were strangers and pilgrims on the Earth. (King James Bible online.org/Bible-verses-About-Aliens/)

Isaiah 60:8, Who are these that fly as clouds and as the doves to their windows?

Ephesians 6:12, For we wrestle not against flesh and blood, but powers, against the rulers of the darkness of this world, against spiritual wickedness in high places.

Colossians 1:16, For by God were all things created, that are in Heaven, and that are in Earth, visible and invisible, whether they be thrones or dominions or principalities, or powers: all things were created by him, and for Him:

Acts 19:35, And when the town-clerk had appeased the people, he said, Ye men of Ephesus, what man is there that knoweth not how that the city of the Ephesians is a worshipper of the goddess Diana, and of the image which fell down from Jupiter? (Bible Verses About Aliens) (KingJamesBibleonline.org)

20

ARE EXTRATERRESTRIAL ALIENS VISITING EARTH?

L evels of belief are often based on proof as it applies to assessing the evidence of extraterrestrial visitations. The following five levels of UAP belief were proposed by Dr. Cole Miller, Professor of Astronomy at the University of Maryland:

The True Believer: The phenomenon in question has been established beyond doubt. And no further data or disproof of apparent evidence will make a difference.

The Hopeful Believer: Willing to accept disproof in individual cases but firmly believes in the overall phenomenon.

The Genuinely Neutral Believer: Has yet to make up their mind and thinks that arguments for or against a phenomenon are equally strong.

The Persuadable Skeptic: Thinks that no current evidence for the phenomenon is enough for belief, but if strong enough evidence is presented, they can accept it.

The Entrenched Skeptic: Not only is current evidence inadequate, but no conceivable future evidence would be enough for belief. (Dr. Bob Wenzel Gross)

Neural Development

According to Dr. Garry Nolan, a Professor of Pathology at Stanford University, neural development sometimes results in an over-connection of neurons deep within the brain's cerebral hemispheres. Dr. Nolan and his team found that the basal ganglia structure in the brains of individuals (experiencers of ET/UFOs) who reportedly witnessed a UAP was different from the brain structure found in the average person.

The basal ganglia are an assembly of subcortical components associated with functions such as voluntary motor control, procedural learning, habit learning, conditional learning, cognition, intuition, and emotion. Individuals who were born with these differences had experiences with ETs/UFOs. All these individuals were high-functioning people. (Dr. Garry Nolan)

What if researchers found that the truth about extraterrestrials wasn't "out there" but in our minds? People with these ET experiences seem to accept these bizarre events without being real (outside the brain). Harvard University Psychiatrist John Mack once hinted that UFO/ET abductions were possibly a physical event fused with a psychological experience. In my experiences with abductions, I must admit that the experience of abduction is made up of three components; a physical event, a psychological experience, and a spiritual experience that results in fear and electrically charged euphoria. My ET experiences were made up of these feelings, and Dr. Nolan is correct in his assessment. Dr. Bob Gross believes that ET/UFO experiences broaden our consciousness and thinking. Anomalous phenomena force us to grow and open us to realities not limited to the physical world but of otherworldly possibilities. (Dr. Bob Wenzel Gross)

Angels And Aliens ET: Is There A Heavenly Relationship?

As I discussed early in this book, the Biblical view held that angels were "from above" yet were essentially humanlike and not, as a rule, invisible. Saint Thomas Aquinas said angels were "pure souls" lacking human bodies. Lactantius, a Christian apologist, wrote in the third century A.D., argued for a principle of relativity: compared to humans, angels are immaterial, but concerning God, angels appeared embodied. Thus, these angel descriptions might be said to possess 'subtle bodies." Are these "subtle bodies" being witnessed by ET abductees who frequently describe the abducting aliens as "ephemeral" creatures whose physical shape is often transient and shifts from material (solid) to immaterial (invisible)? As reported by ET abductees, these entities can walk through walls and float through windows. If so, then we have one easily observable correlation. But many other correlations in this book will come later.

Researcher and author Zechariah Sitchin, whose five-part series "The Earth Chronicles" is considered a classic of ancient astronaut-type research, also grapples with our traditional concepts of what angels are and how they appear. Sitchin wrote in his recent book "Divine Encounters, A Guide to Visions, Angels, and other Emissaries" (Avon, 1995), Sitchin tells us, "The Popular notion of angels, an image sustained and bolstered by centuries of religious art, is that of fully anthropomorphic, humanlike beings who. Unlike people, they are equipped with wings. If they were stripped of their wings, they would look human.

Earlier we read that angels did not have the wings that most religions are said to have claimed. This does get confusing when you consider Sitchin's studies in the Sumerian Anunnaki culture that existed around twenty-five hundred BCE. This race of giant people in Mesopotamia was considered highly intelligent and was teaching humans writing skills. They also said they helped create humans into the modern-day Homosapien we are today. Their culture could very well go as far back as sixty thousand years. These Anunnaki, ancient

Sumerians, were depicted with wings in wall carvings. If angels did not have wings, these Anunnaki would have had flying apparatuses attached to their backs for flight.

Sitchin continues, Western iconography, brought back by early Christianity," was "the undoubted origin of such a representation of angels was the ancient Near East. Where the angels were depicted with wings, this art form was found in Sumerian art-the winged emissary who led Enkidu (an ancient Sumerian deity) away, the guardians with the deadly beams. This same art form of winged humanoids was found in the religious art of Assyria and Egypt, Canaan, and Phoenicia. Hittite contact representations were even duplicated in South America, on the Gate of the Sun in Tiahuanaco-evidence of Hittite contacts with that distant place. If these winged humanoid beings were seen in other cultures worldwide, advanced forms of transportation would be involved in connecting cultures thousands of miles apart. Sitchin avoided religious connotations and referred to the depicted beings as "protective geniuses," the ancient peoples considered them to be a class of lesser gods, rank-and-file divine beings that only carried out orders of the "Great Lords." Their representation as winged beings.

In the story in the Bible, Genesis 18, about Sodom and Gomorrah, the homosexuals wanted to have intercourse with the two angels that appeared to Abraham in the terebinths of Mamre. It is unlikely that the men of Sodom would have a sexual interest in the angels had they been semi-transparent, glowing apparitions with wings and halos! These two angels were described as having the appearance of men. Could these humanoid angels have been extraterrestrials that come in the form of human angels? We can start seeing the confusion between angels and extraterrestrials.

One of the New Testament stories I have always been fascinated with was about the two angels who were confused as to be men at the empty tomb of Jesus after the resurrection. Luke the Apostle stated, "And it came to pass, as they were much perplexed thereabout, behold, two men stood by them in shining garments" (Luke 24:4). After Jesus ascended into Heaven, the disciples looked on. "And while they steadfastly looked toward Heaven as he went up, behold, two men stood by them in white apparel" (Acts 1:10). These "two men" were angels with physical bodies who advised the disciples that Jesus would return "in like manner." This story by Luke could be confused with extraterrestrials as the manlike angels that assisted Jesus in ascending to Heaven or up to something else. (Angels And Aliens: Is There A Heavenly Relationship?)

Angels Could Be an Alien Race Ignored By Science

Throughout the Bible, it is shown how angels had conversations with humans in earthly languages. It is expected that, as extraterrestrial beings, angels have a form of communication different from the languages of Earth. In reading the Bible thoroughly, we find different interpretations hence different religions. It is said in the Scriptures that if you remain silent, God will speak to you. That is true in the accounts that I have experienced. Does this mean it is telepathic communication that God is transmitting to us? The extraterrestrial beings also communicate through telepathic means in most all ET abductions that have been documented. Could this be the language the Biblical Prophets are talking about?

In Isaiah 55:9, God said that His "ways and thoughts" are superior to those of humans, which includes His language, as we read in this chapter. In his letter to the Corinthians, the apostle Paul who claimed to have had direct contact with angels made a distinction between the "tongues of men" and the "tongues of angels." This scripture text denotes that angels have a language that does not belong to human nature. So, angelic creatures not only communicate with each other in a different language, but such language is beyond the learning capacity of humans.

In the Bible, it is said by Paul that angels have their language. What would that language be like? One answer might be the visions recorded in several parts of the New Testament; when fully in a lucid dream state, people contemplated images impossible to recreate. These events are like the effects of a process known as transcranial magnetic stimulation (TMS), which is utilized to introduce images into the human mind through electromagnetic radiation. In my experience, I call it dumbed down by electromagnetism, where you can't speak or move except to only utilize your eyes for seeing. This same energy can produce lucid dreams, either regressed in subconscious dreams or implanted by a higher intelligence. (10 Reasons Angels Could Be an Alien Race Ignored By Science-Listverse)

Angels could be Protecting Our Universe in Secret

In recent years, scientists have discovered that a mysterious force called "dark energy" accelerates the universe's expansion; dark energy decreases or increases depending on the moment, defying even well-known physical laws. This force "plays" with the universal structure, and the scientific community still does not understand exactly what this energetic manifestation is about.

In the Biblical text of Job 38:31, God asks His servant, "Shall you be able to join together the shining stars of the Pleiades?" Within this context, the Creator affirms that He is the one who maintains the order of the universe at will, and only God can modify it as necessary.

The Holy Scriptures also state that angels can control natural elements at their discretion. Could angels be the so-called dark energy that baffles scientists and controls cosmic expansion? It is not clear that the angels manipulate dark energy, but if so, that would explain the unknown force that shapes the universe's fluctuations almost deliberately. Maybe the angels are helping keep the universe in order with the material universe, and we don't even know it. Also, is it possible that extraterrestrials can manipulate dark energy for their use in traveling from star to star and maybe Galaxy to Galaxy? One day we might know the answers to the universe's mysteries and gain the ability to traverse other planetary systems.

Biblical Chapter number 22 tells of the story of a man named Balaam (discussed earlier), who, by order of a foreign King, was going to curse the army of Israel. When he met the King, an angel got in his way and would not let him pass. Balaam blamed the animal he was riding on without seeing the angel and hit it. The angel suddenly became visible in front of the man, and then Balaam understood the seriousness of the matter.

Hearing these stories of angels being invisible in the Bible, it would seem these angelic creatures prefer to observe human actions in secret. They were hidden in plain sight, but we don't know their presence. Their superior physical ability allows them to enter or leave the visible spectrum. Our modern scientists have been working on invisibility cloaking for some time now. They have discovered several ways to achieve invisibility and are close to developing a usable form of cloaking. This could be a possible back-engineered technology of extraterrestrial races that visit Earth. Extraterrestrials are known (especially from my experiences) to cloak their ships (UFOs) and even walk around in your house invisible by cloaking their bodies. This is one of the attributes that angels and extraterrestrials share that makes it challenging to identify and confusing to know which is an ET or an angel.

Objects can become invisible, for example, by covering them with layers of materials (specifically called "metamaterials") capable of bending light or by making it resonate at specific frequencies using electromagnetic waves. If invisibility is possible with humans, it is evident that angels could also develop an ability of that kind. Since angels existed long before humans, it is possible that angels had these abilities millions of years ago. God is the angels' source of all spiritual energy, and God can produce anything supernatural with his all-powerful, all-knowing intelligence.

The Zoo Hypothesis

Getting back to the extraterrestrial behavior and goals, and their purpose of visiting and watching us humans. A scientific formulation known as the zoo hypothesis has been talked about in scientific circles and published to the public. This hypothesis suggests that an advanced alien race deliberately avoids contact with humans. Scientists also theorize that extraterrestrials are secretly watching us evolve.

In Job 38:4-7, God explains to His human servant that when the Earth was formed, the angels, described as "morning stars," celebrated with joy at such an event. This Biblical statement shows that angels are creatures different from humans, unique in themselves. Angels have been around long before the emergence of the first human beings on Earth. Throughout Biblical history and religious texts, all sources claim that angels have existed since the beginning. God created angels before any other life form in the universe or universes (plural, maybe eleven universes, as physicists claim).

As we learned in the previous paragraph that extraterrestrials watched us, humans, in secret, and the angels, in the same manner, do not manifest themselves before humans, maybe for the same reason. Everything points to the fact that the angels have been watching us throughout history. Therefore, the angels know human behavior very well. Humans are very predictable to angels since they have known us since our beginnings, so they know how to remain hidden from our sight very well. (10 Reasons Angels Could Be An Alien Race Ignored By Science – Listverse)

The main question of humankind is whether there is life outside our world. We now live in a time when this question of whether other life forms in our universe exist is more openly discussed amongst most scientists. The scientific community has invested hundreds of millions of dollars in finding potentially habitable planets in space, and NASA and the government are spending more. Despite detecting habitable planets, scientists' search for alien life forms is minimal: They plan to identify carbon-based life forms. All life forms known to humans (including us) are carbon-based. So, the reason for using that filter in the search is evident. The problem with using such a tight filter to look for forms like ours is that they will miss other forms of life. Alien life forms made up of different compositions, like silicon, would go unnoticed, including plausible angelic creatures.

While angels are not abstract forces but have bodies, studies on the sacred texts show that angels are represented by nature closer to that of God. In short, angels seem to be life forms composed of an unknown substance, superior to any known type of matter or energy. Angels are made up of unknown substances and characteristics, and scientists would need help to locate this type of being, even with their best technology. Angels and extraterrestrials seem to elude us in their invisible body composition of different substances unknown to us. Sure, they both can materialize momentarily to show us what they look like, but do we know what they look like even when they become visible? Then the Shapeshifting aspect goes into play. The confusion they stir in humans makes them elusive and unnoticeable in our world and frequency ranges.

The Angelic World Is Outside the Visible Universe.

If you ever wanted to know where the "end of space is?" The Bible states that expansion comprises three zones called "Heavens." The first one is our atmosphere, the second Heaven is outer space, and the third is God's dwelling place. At the end of space is God, that surrounds all His universes. God is outside of all our universes and watching over all his creation. The immaterial characteristics attributed to God; it is understood that the last Heaven refers to a place separate from the physical universe. It is said that angels stand before God, so logically, these creatures live in the same divine abode or "Heaven." When angels travel to Earth on a mission from God, they travel great distances to get here. But space and time do not matter to the angels because of their divine supernatural abilities given to them by God. (10 Reasons Angels Could Be An Alien Race Ignored By Science – Listverse)

Extraterrestrials; Fallen Angels or Demonic Beings?

Modern Ufologists cringe at the mention of any angelic/demonic involvement with extraterrestrial sightings and abductions. The bulk of abduction cases provides ample proof that they can be seen within the context of demonic involvement. The ancient stories of angels mating with human females at the dawn of time annoy the believer in extraterrestrial visitors and, of course, the ancient astronaut theorists. The truth and the modern component existing within the UFO phenomenon must be clarified and apparent to the observer. With invisible entities with shapeshifting abilities, in the eyes of the observer, they cannot ascertain precisely what they saw.

Modern Biblical scholars that study extraterrestrial phenomena are theorizing that Fallen Angels are masquerading as "aliens." They believe these extraterrestrial/fallen angels are abducting people to create Nephilim hybrids. Other authors, and even I, think this theory does hold some validity after studying Enoch and the fallen angels' texts in the book of Enoch and Geneses chapter in the Bible. As we discussed earlier in this book, the Nephilim Giants inhabited the Earth after human women gave birth to these hybrid Giants. God vanquished the fallen angels and their offspring to the depths of the Earth, leaving the giants to procreate and flourish. Some giants still could be hiding from us in the deep caves here on Earth, waiting for their time to come out and battle with humans.

Barry Chamish, in his book "Return of the Giants," has documented the phenomena occurring in Israel, which Chamish believes is the returning of Giants to the Land of Israel. "Well over a dozen "alien" visitations have been reported, and many Arabs have even reported seeing demons. Today that number of visits could be many times greater than the visitations of aliens during that time. Seven of the best-documented close encounters with aliens during this time, with alien beings, probably connected to UFOs, six involved giants. These giant aliens left evidence of their arrival in the form of cadmium-imbued landing circles. In addition, the aliens left miles of impossible boot tracks and deliberate communication with witnesses." Dr. Jacques F. Vallee, one of the most renowned UFO researchers, has stated concerning UFO abduction phenomena.

The "medical examinations," to which abductees are said to be subjected, often accompanied by sadistic sexual manipulation, are reminiscent of the medieval tales of encounters with demons. "Any intelligent being equipped with the scientific marvels that UFOs possess would be in a position to achieve any of these alleged scientific objectives in a shorter time and with fewer risks," and that "the symbolic display seen by the abductees is identical to the type of initiation ritual or astral voyage that is imbedded in the (occult) traditions of every culture. The structure of abduction stories is identical to that of occult initiation rituals. The UFO beings of today belong to the same class of manifestation as the (occult) entities described in centuries past." Putting my experiences with abductions in this mix, I can say there was an element of sexual interplay. Still, it was mainly for the extraterrestrials to collect semen and DNA for the hybridizing goals of their race of aliens.

My thoughts are a little different than calling it an occult activity or ritual that the extraterrestrials are performing; it has a purpose for them. They collect these samples from humans to use to create hybrid beings and to monitor our DNA evolution. This biological intervention of us humans by extraterrestrials is to manipulate our DNA to produce a higher intelligence and consciousness level that develops us into a more peaceful human race. (Nephilim Today – timetobelieve.com)

Today, you can see in our news media and the military reports that they are admitting UFOs/UAPs exist and are studying them. The truth is that the government has been studying UFOs for fifty years.

In recent years, the reports of UFOs have skyrocketed! The increasing number of UFO sightings is giving way to an alarming number of troubling things emerging on the horizon. Each UFO sighting pushes us closer to a call for full disclosure by our government and military.

The military will not fully disclose the presence of UFOs because I think the extraterrestrials are also making that decision behind closed doors to the public. Our visitors feel we are not ready for a world meeting with them because our consciousness is not high enough – meaning being open-minded about their existence. Most people think religions will crumble and fall apart due to full UFO disclosure and challenge their religious principles. As we read earlier, the Holy Bible has scripture that does not deny other Heavenly life forms. The Church might be more accepting of full disclosure because society has been inundated with UFO sightings. Our modern-day cell phones can take pictures on the spot instantly and have helped create good evidence.

And for this cause, the Lord shall send them strong delusion, that they should believe a lie (2Thess. 2:3).

Where is the deception, but where do the fallen angels operate? What is this strong delusion? They said in the scriptures that the fallen angels would once again come to Earth as "star gods," but they have yet to appear as of this date! That is a great delusion. They are from another realm, not from a planet. These fallen angels will have their leader (ambassador), the Antichrist, for they are the beast of the Apocalypse. Most people think that the end time is coming soon because of the world chaos and the increased UFO sightings. (timeto-believe.com)

Our scientists are producing hybrids in their secret laboratories and facilities worldwide. In most countries, it is illegal to produce hybrid humans or creatures, chimeras. "A significant adjunct or supplement to the primary and only means known to fallen angels of producing a first-generation Nephilim-hybrid is ekporneuo (gross fornication – Jude 6-7)! The Bible scripture states, which corroborates what the witnesses of this abduction phenomena have consistently reported, which is at the heart of Jesus' prophecy." (Matt. 24:37 & Luke 17:26-27) – Doug Riggs

Future Incursions

The war between good and evil is real. The forces of the fallen angels have been warring against humankind since the dawn of history. The fallen angels have been called many names, our names that fall short of describing their malevolence. These fallen angels (evil-doers) have forever manipulated us to our demise. In every turning point in history, they have been working on a plan known only to themselves. These fallen angels, evildoers, are associated with the shadow government, Cabal, deep state, and corrupt leaders as dictators. Corrupt politicians succumb to these evil plans of the fallen angels by taking bribes for monetary reward. As the Bible states, money could be the root of all evil. In modern times, evil is a dictator starting wars with innocent people and sending thousands of soldiers to their deaths, like in the Russia and Ukraine war. We don't know whom these shadowy people run the world governments. We can only guess that maybe they are the ancient evil fallen angels in charge of all the death and destruction on this planet.

There have been discussions throughout our human history of the end-of-the-world scenarios posed by Biblical scriptures, prophets, and religious leaders in the Church. People get the general feeling at times in our past and the present day that the end is near. Biblical scriptures state that only our Lord God knows the day and time the end will happen. They say, "a storm is gathering," meaning humans feel the end is coming subconsciously feeling this bad energy. There is a theory that the Nephilim (fallen angels) are mating with humans in our present time, creating modern-day Nephilim. We approach the inescapability of this coming Apocalypse, unaware and unarmed against the Nephilim, which are hybrids, alive in history and today, fathered by the Watchers. It is claimed that the Nephilim (fallen angels) appear in UFOs and alien abductions. They use the extraterrestrial UFO appearance to deceive humankind into believing they are from distant stars, calling themselves Star Gods.

Statements like, "Soon the Apocalypse will be upon us, and even darker beings will walk among us!" If you read Dr. David Jacobs's book "They Walk Amongst Us," he describes that the extraterrestrials or Nephilim are already here and have been with us throughout the whole of human history. In my experiences, I have met strange aliens that did not appear to fit into our environment. If you can believe that opinion about the Nephilim, these extraterrestrials or Nephilim are worth looking at, but I feel there are many species of extraterrestrials in our universe. Some Ufologists and scientists agree that four to six different ET races communicate with top government and military people. It has been said that President Truman, Eisenhower, and Nixon met with these extraterrestrial beings. In their meetings, they deliberated on nuclear warfare that the extraterrestrials did not want, agreed upon high technology exchanges, and disclosure coordination in which it is said that the ETs are holding up announcing full disclosure. They want our human society to have more consciousness and acceptance of them. (Nephilim Today – timetobelieve.com)

21

HUMAN CONFUSION OF EXTRATERRESTRIALS AND ANGELS

S ome researchers say there might be a connection between UFOs and angel sightings. However, most scientists and some Bible scholars feel that the angels and Heavenly figures encountered in the Bible might have been extraterrestrials. Some of what we have learned from Biblical scripture in this book points to the strong possibility that angels were misinterpreted as spiritual entities while, all along, they could have been extraterrestrials since their shapeshifting and invisibility characteristics were of the same supernatural powers being demonstrated.

In 2002, Guy Malone interviewed with "The History Channel" TV network to discuss UFOs in the Bible. He looked at key Biblical angels with aliens and other similar beings from various cultures. The popular belief is that angels are spoken about throughout the Bible; there are only twenty-four actual mentions in the Old Testament. The Old Testament references specify the "Angel of the Lord," another way of saying that God has appeared as an angel, so not in reality. It is not common for an angel to appear as a physical manifestation. Angels are likelier to show themselves in a dream, trance, or vision. Evidence in the Bible suggests an angel can induce a trance state to bring interesting questions when viewed concerning stories of abductions by extraterrestrials.

Angels appear fewer than fifty times across the Bible, certainly not hundreds of times. An angel might have appeared in a room, walked through a wall, or teleported into the room from another dimension or Heaven, as ancients called it. Similarly, telepathy and mindreading are not mentioned in the Bible, as it is frequently involved in extraterrestrial visits and abductions. I have been visited by ETs, who used electrical energy to immobilize me, leaving me with only visual abilities. Extraterrestrials use magnetic energy to take control of your mind and body, but ancient people would not know how to describe that energy or feeling. They would say they were in a trance, as the Bible states. Those that report aliens today do not describe angels mentioned in the Bible. These alien sightings are not operating in the service of God and so cannot be classed as the same kind of angel equivalent.

According to the Bible, angels appear in human form. They are beautiful so as not to scare their human contact. The opposite with alien visitors also appearing in humanoid form. Most always, they are reported as being ugly. Mostly reptilian in appearance. Yes, this author saw a reptilian and a little grey ET. Very seldom will an ET witness report the humanoid appearance as looking like a tall blonde attractive Nordic-looking alien, but these are not the norm. Aliens will appear in tight space suits or without any clothing. And it has been reported that aliens also wear white robes that shine brightly and glow. The type of symbols seen by contactees during an alien's visit is more likely occult or pagan symbolism. Angels will appear for a specific reason as assigned by God for intervention with their human contact to give instructions. It will also be a short visit made by angels; after they are done, they leave quickly. Aliens often constantly make contact for years and hang around longer with their subject contactee. The knowledge the aliens impart is telepathically uploaded to a person's subconscious, and the memory is erased. Never have I heard from a contactee or me that they say Jesus was a hybrid or a self-realized human. I can't entirely agree with the idea that ETs impart religious or divine information. It is more like conscious aspects of the universe.

Angels are so adaptive at changing into human form that even the Bible acknowledges that we may be in the presence of an angel and not know it. Angels can look wholly human, and that is how they can get close to us and gain our trust in what they will instruct us to do. Many say that an angel looks very human when they see it. Angels can appear as beautiful humans, so people seek them out as sexual partners. According to Hebrews 1:14, Biblical angels are sent to assist those who are in times of need. Particularly those who are followers of God or those that will become followers. Again, I disagree that aliens teach occultism and new-age spirituality and lead their victims to UFO cults. Never have I heard an abductee talk about UFO cults or new-age teachings, and I have interviewed many abductees. And, for my own experiences with extraterrestrials, never have I been taught to believe in any occult. As an abductee, you hardly remember anything they telepathically tell you.

Angels can shapeshift into any form of human body or animal form. This is also attributed to aliens that can shapeshift into any form they want. Women abductees report being sexually abused and undergo medical procedures to remove reproductive eggs by aliens. Some women get pregnant and have apparent miscarriages three months later. This is because the aliens return for the hybrid baby and take it back. In contrast, the Biblical angels seek to help people with their medical problems and distress. My experiences with extraterrestrials have demonstrated that they all are not "fallen angels" but different species of alien life forms across our universe, at least fifty-seven races of ETs. (The Rhodium Rule – p/c Jacob Meissner)

Bible Mysteries that could be explained by Aliens

Blaze's "Ancient Aliens" touches on the idea of aliens making their presence known in the Bible. We will look at several Biblical stories again to further explain the alien and angel connection. In the Good Book, we will discuss a few stories in the Bible that aliens could have played a part.

Were the Nephilim giant extraterrestrials?

Earlier in this book, I spoke about the fallen angels and the mating with human women to produce hybrid offspring. So, they brought to the Israelites an unfavorable report of the land they had spied on, saying, "The land that we have gone through as spies for the people that we saw in it are of great size. There we saw the Nephilim, and to ourselves, we seemed like grasshoppers incapable of destroying them. (Numbers 13:32-33) According to the books of Genesis, Numbers, and Ezekial, the "Nephilim" were a group of enigmatic and mysterious "people" of quite a large stature. They were regarded by many as supernatural in origin. In the Bible, we compare angels and aliens in this story. Some Biblical scholars believe the Nephilim were demons or fallen angels; others say they may have been aliens. Or, at least, part alien and human hybrid, anyway. The theory exists that suggests these enormous beings were alien-human hybrids. The product of Nephilim (fallen angels) and human women that looked to be eight meters high at their tallest. Tales of these giants originate across almost all the lands, which lends credence to their existence. It remains to be proven if they have been from outer space.

The Spaceships of Ezekiel

Then I looked, and behold, a whirlwind was coming out of the north, a great cloud with raging fire engulfing itself, and brightness was all glowing of amber from the midst of the fire. Also, from within came the likeness of four living creatures. And this was their appearance: they had four heads; a lion, an ox, an eagle, and a man. And each one had four wings. Ezekiel 1:4-6, Ezekiel had a vision of the Throne-Chariot (1:4-28), which sees the prophet; Ezekiel had a vision no other prophet has ever had. This can be compared to modern UFO/alien sightings. It is not just the ancient alien types who believe and buy into this UFO theory. In 1974, the esteemed and respected NASA engineer Josef F. Blumrich wrote that Ezekiel's vision was, in fact, that of a visiting alien spacecraft. (Bible mysteries that could be explained by Aliens/BLAZE TV)

Was Noah an Alien?

Noah was famous in the Bible for Noah's ark story in (Genesis 5:29) when he saved a male and female of every species on Earth, including his family, from the great flood. God destroyed the world because the giants (Nephilim) were evil and disobeyed his commands. He wanted Noah to cleanse the world of sinful giants and people and to carry on humanity. God instructed Noah to build an ark large enough to hold two of every kind of lifeform. Noah's giant wooden boat was the only extraordinary thing about the man. In (Genesis 6:11-9:19) it was said that Noah's father was Lamech, and his mother was Ninth. Noah was from the Enoch bloodline, an ancient family lineage filled with mystery and supernatural events.

According to the famous Dead Sea Scrolls, young Noah had 'glowing' skin as a baby and could light up a room with his eyes. He also had ashen skin, unlike his fellow tribe members with olive-colored skin. Noah was known to be very tall by the scribes who wrote the Dead Sea Scrolls—making Noah's actual father appear to be an alien and his mother a human woman. Bible Scholars ask themselves, was Noah's father from another planet? Noah's earlier ancestors, Enoch and Methuselah (died the very year of the great flood at 969 years old), the oldest man to ever live on Earth. Noah was also a descendant of Adam, and Adam of the Garden of Eden existed between ninety-nine thousand and one hundred forty-eight thousand years ago. We are all descendants of Adam in the overall DNA line. According to the Bible, the Earth is only six thousand years old, and we know that figure is wrong. Could these Biblical accounts be talking about non-human aliens living hundreds of years in their life span? If this story is all true, then these ancient early Biblical figures were superhuman and not of this Earth. Some ancient alien theorists suggest that would explain Noah's ethereal appearance and even communicated with God directly about dealing with the Great Flood (he was a higher being and did not carry the sin that other humans did). (Bible mysteries that could be explained by aliens/BLAZE TV)

A Christian Perspective of Angels and Aliens

Travis Perry (Speculative Faith articles) says that the idea that holds aliens and angels are the same: 1) Both are imaginary, 2) Both are spiritual, and 3) Both are extraterrestrial. Travis thinks all three ideas, while interesting, need to be corrected.

Travis continues to say he believes in the reality of the spiritual realm and accepts the Biblical descriptions of angels. He says that there are quite a lot of details about angels that the Bible never addresses. Travis says that aliens existing on other planets in our physical universe would not be the same as angels. One is physical, and one is spiritual. He mentions that aliens may or may not exist, but he believes they may be entities in our universe. Most Christians do not believe that aliens can exist, a topic that is ever-changing in modern times with many more sightings. Travis says that if aliens did exist, such life would have been created by God, just as God created life on Earth. This author entirely agrees with this statement that God made other life forms in the vast expanse of our universe. They say that we must be very selfish to think that God only created human beings.

Travis Perry mentions a story by Grace Bridges equating aliens and angels in the world of AE she created but instead, she played with perceived similarities. In that story, she has story arcs that mention human beings worshipping the-aliens-partially-confused-with-angels in her anthology set in this world that I (Travis) helped edit. He says this would realistically happen and would be interesting to see the effects on human beings who met aliens who thought they were angels, even though they are not angels. (Speculative Faith articles: Travis Perry)

Since God creates all life-like alien races, wouldn't they have accounts of a creator God and fall into sin and redemption? And Heavenly beings serve God but resemble aliens, literally "alien angels." What would they look like? What would happen if we humans met alien angels? I am sure that with the technology and millions of years ahead of humans, they would better understand God and His supernatural powers. Aliens could not escape God's energies that create all things, and I am sure they abide by the rules of God's all-mighty powers. Or could it be that one creator God would retain a whole entirely different set of Heavenly beings for this other purpose? These aliens are not directly mentioned in the Bible because we humans don't "need to know" about them. What would a relationship be like between human angels and alien angels? Would they battle each other as they did thousands of years ago like the fallen angels fought the angels of God? Maybe that is precisely what happened. God's angels fought the sinful or fallen angels to keep the Earth cleansed of sin and Satan's army of fallen angels from taking over the humans on Earth.

Wouldn't it be interesting if some alien angel – or alien rather like an angel, resembled something we think of as evil but was not evil? My experiences with ETs and talking to other abductees say they had spiritual feelings of elation, not torture or horror, as evil aliens would perform on humans. (Travis Perry)

It is interesting what Travis Perry says about aliens. He does not claim to know the reality behind stories of alien encounters and abductions. Travis said he agrees with Carl Sagan that if alien species were to travel all this way to Earth – which is not easy to do according to the best human understanding of the science of interstellar travel. The aliens would not likely be content with random captures of lost truck drivers in remote areas and people like that. What did he mean by that statement? He says the typically poor person would not make a good abductee and a prize finding for the aliens. I find that a little discriminatory. Again, he says he does not know what the alien's thinking is about when it comes to abductions. The primary characteristic of aliens is that they are supposed to be different from human beings and do strange things we would not do ourselves.

In all my experiences with the abduction phenomena, I have met people of all socio-economical classes that had experiences with ETs. Myself? I was an impoverished young kid who saw a UFO with a friend, and we were abducted. Why would they be interested in a boy that had to put cardboard in his shoe soles to cover the holes? It is not your money, or social class like Travis was alluding to that poor people would not be a good specimen for aliens. He is right, and he knows nothing about ET behavior at all, and neither did Carl Sagan. They both sound like stuffed-shirted men with better-than-thou attitudes.

Sure, the fallen angels are now operating in the spiritual realm – and yes, the human imagination and hysterical hallucination, not to mention hoaxes, could be part of this phenomenon of alien visitations along with abductions that could be a product of a bad dream. This author has seen and felt many supernatural experiences, but I also had witnesses. This skeptical approach this author shows is not suitable for the research and investigation of ET incidents. Is this a product of religious dogma with blinders on not accepting people's UFO and ET experiences? There is much uncertainty in this author Travis' written word. He thinks demons are more responsible for abductions than aliens.

If you can believe in demons that either abduct or possess people, why doesn't he believe in aliens? Are there hoaxes and hallucinations? Yes! About twenty percent of ET reports can be considered hoaxes by people with motives of being famous and getting their fifteen minutes of fame. Some experiencers may think their abductions were real, but on the contrary, they were bad dreams. This is a small percentage of people with false stories. What about all those with real detailed facts and witnesses to back them up and their experiences? I am one of those experiencers with witnesses and details to support my ET events. Lies change; truth stays the same no matter how often you tell it. Consistent truth is the quality I look for in an abductee's story. (Travis Perry)

Another point of view worth mentioning: is the "ancient alien" perspective, the notion that aliens came to Earth in ancient times and were mistaken for spiritual beings. When the Bible talks about Heavenly creatures, these creatures "really" were aliens. We are going back and forth believing aliens and people's intervention. In ancient times didn't these same Heavenly creatures visit with the poor commoners? Barry Downing, in 1968, wrote "The Bible and Flying Saucers," in which he laid out his idea. He also claimed that Jesus was an extraterrestrial, eventually called up to "Heaven" by a UFO. The description that Ezekiel gave in the Bible of the aliens' appearance seemed to have some credence. But when the aliens (Heavenly creatures) spoke to Ezekiel concerning morality and the religious practices of ancient Israel, it would not make sense coming from aliens. Still, Ezekiel's explanation of what the UFO and aliens looked like would be more probable than what the aliens told him. I agree with this author on this aspect of Ezekiel's experience written in the Bible. This author's statement sounds skeptical of Ezekiel's UFO experience regarding physical observations and the words the aliens told him. (Speculative Faith Articles: Travis Perry 2019)

22

THE REAL SUPERNATURAL BEINGS WE NEED TO PROTECT AGAINST

THE DEVIL, SATAN, AND LUCIFER – WHO ARE THEY?

Lucifer

In the Book of Isaiah, chapter 14, the King of Babylon is condemned in a prophetic vision by the prophet Isaiah and is called (Helel ben Shachar, Hebrew for "shining one, son of the morning"), who is called (Helel ben Sahar). The title "Helel ben Sahar" refers to the planet Venus as the morning star; that is how the Hebrew word is usually interpreted. Helel, or Heylel, occurs only once in the Hebrew Bible. The Septuagint renders in Greek as (heosphoros), bringer of dawn." The ancient Greek name for the morning star. The Vulgate renders Lucifer, the word in that language for the morning star in Latin. According to the King James Bible-based Strong's Concordance, the original Hebrew means: shining one, light-bearer," also, in the King James Bible, it is named planet Venus, "Lucifer," as it was in the Wycliffe Bible.

The translation of the word "Lucifer" has been abandoned in modern English translations of Isaiah 14:12. Present-day translations render Lucifer as the "morning star" (New International Version, New Century Version, New American Standard Bible, Contemporary

English Version, Common English Bible, and complete Jewish Bible, The Message,) "Day Star, or "shining one," or "shining star" (New Living Translation). In the modern translation from the original Hebrew, the passage in which the phrase "Lucifer" or "morning star" occurs begins with the statement: "On the day the Lord gives you relief from your suffering and turmoil and the harsh labor forced on you, you will take this taunt against the King of Babylon: How the oppressor has come to an end! How his fury has ended!" After the death of the King, the taunt continues: (Lucifer – Wikipedia)

How you have fallen from Heaven, morning star, son of the dawn! You have been cast down to Earth, who once laid the nations low! You said in your heart, "I will ascend to the Heavens; I will raise my throne above the stars of God; I will sit enthroned on the mount of assembly, on the utmost heights of Mount Zaphon. "I will ascend to the tops of the clouds; "I will make myself like the most high." Instead, you are brought down to the realm of the dead, to the depths of the pit. Those who look at you and stare ponder your fate: "Is this the man who shook the Earth and made Kingdoms tremble, the man who made the world a wilderness, who overthrew its cities and kept the captives, not letting them leave?" I noticed that the term "man" was used. This person shook the Earth, as it states. Do we have to consider this evil person a human being? Or was he Lucifer?

For the unnamed "King of Babylon," many identifications have been proposed. They included the Babylonian ruler of the prophet Isaiah's own time, the later Nebuchadnezzar II, under whom Babylonian captivity of the Jews began, or Nabonidus, and the Assyrian Kings Tiglath-Pileser, Sargon II, and Sennacherib. Verse twenty says that this King of Babylon will not be "joined with them (all of the Kings of the nations) in burial because thou hast destroyed thy land, slain thy people; the seed of evil-doers shall not be named forever." Herbert Wolf held that the "King of Babylon" was not a specific ruler but a generic representation of the whole line of rulers. Isaiah could have labeled the word Lucifer or evil-doer Kings evil rulers. Are we unsure of the terminology the ancients used to standardize terms for evil people – Luciferian?

Isaiah 14:12 became a source for the popular conception of the fallen angel motif. Rabbinical Judaism has rejected any belief in rebel or fallen angels. In the eleventh century, Rabbi Eliezer illustrates the origin of the "fallen angel myth" by giving two accounts; one relates to the angel in the Garden of Eden who seduces Eve, and the other relates to the angels, the benei elohim who cohabit with the daughters of man (Genesis 6:1-4). An association of (Isaiah 14:12-18) with the personification of evil called the devil developed outside of mainstream Rabbinic Judaism in pseudepigrapha and Christian writings, notably mentioned in talking about the apocalypses. In Biblical references to the meaning of evil by the prophets, there were mixed messages about terminology and the leaning toward an individual's interpretation as they saw it.

Aquila of Sinope derives the Hebrew name for the morning star from the verb yalal (to lament). This derivation was adopted as a proper name for an angel who mourns the loss of his former beauty. The Christian Church Fathers – for example, Hieronymus, in his Vulgate-translated this as Lucifer. In those ancient times, Lucifer was equated with the fallen angels, perceived in the first century Palestinian Judaism. Early Church Fathers brought the fallen Lightbringer Lucifer into the connection with the Devil based on a saying of Jesus in the Gospel of Luke (10:18 EU): " I saw Satan fall from Heaven like lightning." Some Christian writers have applied the name "Lucifer," as used in the Book of Isaiah, and the motif of a Heavenly being cast down to the Earth, to the devil. Sigve K. Tonstad argues the New Testament War in Heaven theme of Revelation 12, in which the dragon "who is called the devil and Satan was thrown down to Earth." Even the Old Testament passages mentioned manifestations of the devil, not any reference to Lucifer. At the time of Latin writer Augustine of Hippo (354-430 A.D.), a contemporary of the composition of the Vulgate, said, "Lucifer had not yet become a common name for the devil."

Augustine of Hippo said that the devil's rebellion was the first cause of evil. Augustine rejects the idea that envy could have been the first sin. Instead, he argues that Lucifer's free will first came into existence. Lucifer's attempt to take God's throne is not an assault on the gates of Heaven but a turn to solipsism in which the devil becomes the God of his world.

The King of Babel uttered his phrase to Isaiah; he was speaking through the spirit of Lucifer, the head of devils. Everybody that falls away from God Isaiah says they are within Lucifer's body and the devil. It seems to add more confusion about whom Lucifer is, especially with different scholars and ancient prophets confusing the devil, Satan, and Lucifer as all the same. Augustine said that the

Earth was already created before the fallen angel (the devil) fell to Earth. He is saying that the fallen angel or angels fell after God created the world. More confusing, right? (Lucifer – Wikipedia)

The name Lucifer is Latin. Translated to English, it would be rendered "light bringer" or "light bearer."

With all these ancient texts and Isaiah's interpretation, it is almost certain that the devil's name is not Lucifer; we did not know Satan's name when he was an angel in Heaven. The name confusion came about between the devil and Lucifer because of an early mistranslated Hebrew scripture in Isaiah 14:12, which had nothing to do with Satan but was discussing a King of Babylon, likely Nebuchadnezzar. One of his titles was "morning star" in Hebrew, which a translator converted into the Latin Lucifer, which translated to English reads "light bringer or bearer," not "morning star." (Isaiah 14:12 King James Bible) ("Lucifer was the bringer of light"? – Quora)

Lucifer is the Prometheus of Christian mythology. In both cases, you have some member of the Heavenly realm bringing humankind the spark of understanding. Prometheus brought fire, symbolizing knowledge; Lucifer led Eve to the tree of knowledge. The "light" in "light bearer" is the light of understanding. This is the essence that separates humans from animals. This makes humans closer to God or the gods. The act of giving humans understanding made the gods or God happy. This act of teaching knowledge to humankind was beneficial to humans. (Ted Wrigley) (Do Christians consider knowledge (light)

Devil and Satan Terminology

Our discussion of Isaiah's metaphor of the morning star in (Isaiah 14:12) which applied to the King of Babylon, gave rise to the general use of the Latin word for "morning star," capitalized as the original name of the devil before his fall from grace. Isaiah 14:12 was linked with Luke 10 ("I saw Satan fall like lightning from Heaven"). This interpretation of the passage in Isaiah is an allegory of Satan's fall from Heaven.

Samael (Hebrew: Samael, "Venom/Poison of God"; Arabic: Samsama 'il or Samail; Samil, or Samiel) is an archangel in Talmudic and post-Talmudic lore; a figure who is the accuser or adversary. Satan, as mentioned in the book of Job, is a seducer and destroyer (Mashhit mentioned in the Book of Exodus). Many of Satan's functions resemble the Christian notion that they identify him as the fallen angel; he is not necessarily evil since Satan's duties are also regarded as good, such as destroying sinners.

Samael, in Midrashic texts, is a member of the Heavenly host with often grim and destructive duties. One of Samael's most significant roles in Jewish lore is that of the main angel of death and the head of Satan. So, another name enters the evil devil/Satan category as Samael. Notice the mention of Satan as plural? That would insinuate that an army of Satan does the destructive work. Although he condones the sins of humans, he remains one of God's servants. In reading the details of these ancient texts, the ordinary human would blame the devil/satan for anything wrong that would happen to them.

Samael frequently appears in the Garden of Eden story and engineers Adam and Eve's fall. The serpent or snake used to convince Eve to bite the apple of knowledge in the Garden of Eve story was Satan himself. Or Samael, Lucifer, or the devil shapeshifted into the serpent. There are several names for evil, depending on your interpretation. However, here is a twist, the snake is not a form of Samael, but a beast he rode like a camel. In a single mention, Samael was believed to be the father of Cain, Eve's son. Samael was also mentioned in the Bible as a partner of Lilith, Adam's first wife, who disobeyed Adam and left the Garden of Eden. Lilith turned out to be an evil woman that was noted to spread misery through her evil character. In early Talmudic and Midrashic literature, he is not identified with Satan yet. Only in later Midrashim is he entitled "head of all the satans." (Samael – Wikipedia)

In Rome, they called Samael, a guardian angel, and he was turned into the archenemy of Israel. By the beginning of Jewish culture in Europe, Samael had been established as a representative of Christianity due to his connection and identification with Rome. In some Gnostic texts, Samael's role as the source of evil became identified with the Demiurge, the creator of the material world. Both accounts originate from the same source. However, the Gnostic development differs from the Jewish development of Samael, in which he is merely an angel and servant of God.

Samael was first mentioned in the Second Temple Period and immediately after its destruction. He was also mentioned in the Book of Enoch, along with other rebellious angels or fallen angels, since Enoch's period speaks a lot about the fallen angels. Samael was considered one of the Watchers who descended to Earth to copulate with human women, although he was never a leader of the fallen angels. Like Enoch, Samael, and other Watchers had long lives, whose bloodlines stretched thousands of years.

In the Greek Apocalypse of Baruch, Samael is the dominant evil figure. Samael plants a knowledge tree; then, God banishes and curses him. Then Samael tempts Adam and Eve into sin by taking the form of the serpent. He appears further as the embodiment of evil in the Ascension of Isaiah, often called: "King of evil, "King of the wicked"). (Samael – Wikipedia)

In ancient mythology and Biblical scriptures, Satan, the devil, and now Samael are all considered evil doers against humankind. Isaiah added Lucifer's name to the Kings of Babylon and gave them an evil persona for their actions against the people. Who has the main title of evil incarnate? Was it Samael? Isaiah mentioned in the ancient texts several possibilities of evil-doers, but did he mean Satan? If Samael was the main culprit in convincing Eve to sin, then he was a shapeshifter reptilian that turned into a serpent. He also managed to impregnate Eve with his son Cain. Cain was part reptilian (extraterrestrial being), making him evil in spirit. This conclusion is this author's opinions and through self-experiences and not a Biblical principle and not written in scripture in the Book of Genesis. But shapeshifting was mentioned in scriptures, and angels (fallen angels) could change into anybody they wanted or needed to help accomplish their mission, either good or bad.

Drawing a comparison between angels and extraterrestrials is a touchy unproven pseudoscience. Same for the intentions of their visits, are they evil (Satan, Devil, and even Luciferian)? Or are they benevolent with good intentions like the God-directed angels with good spiritual intent? We can see that even Isaiah and the early Christian followers could not discern the difference. In ancient times the devil and Satan were called fallen angels, or they referred to the Nephilim giants, as in the Book of Enoch, as evil. Biblical scholars and modern-day scientists are still trying to determine when the various so-called names for evil were given and mentioned by humans. We could be talking six thousand years ago or eight hundred eighty years ago. The Great Flood happened around (1880 BCE) in and around Mesopotamia (Genesis 7:11-12). Noah was six hundred and one years old at the time of the flood and lived until he died when he was nine hundred and fifty years old (Genesis 9:28-29). It was strange that Noah lived almost a thousand years old, so he could not have been an average human. Are we talking about Noah and his bloodline of Enoch being extraterrestrial in nature? The longevity of humans and the Bible years mentioned in scripture still confuse scientists today. Evil started before the Great Flood with the serpent in the Garden of Eden, estimated in the Bible as fifteen hundred and fifty years before the Great Flood. Biblical dates (Genesis 5:3) and (Genesis 7:6).

Satan, or the Devil, is one of the best-known characters in Western Jewish, Christianity, and Islam traditions. Surprisingly, the entity was a latecomer in the ancient world. As an evil being, Satan is nowhere to be found in the Jewish Bible. He evolved during the height of the

Persian Achaemenid Empire (beginning in 550 BCE) and was adopted by Jews living under Persian rule. His formal name, Satan, derives from the Hebrew 'ha-satan', 'Ha' means 'the,' and Satan means 'opposer' or 'adversary.' The opposer of God's creation. Greek 'diabolos,' English 'devil,' meant 'accuser,' 'slanderer,' again describing his role. The concept of Satan emerged over time in phases. It is confusing when and where these names that indicate evil-doers happened in the Biblical sense. (Article – Rebecca Denova 2021)

In (Deuteronomy 28), God declares that he controls prosperity and suffering. Many creation myths addressed how and why evil arose. Evil has always existed. Humans encountered natural disasters (earthquakes, floods, wars with pillage and rape, disease, plagues, infant mortality, man-made evil such as murders and theft, and of course, death). As the ancient people developed their religious systems, the existence of evil had to be explained and rationalized. When good things happened, they gave God credit for delivering them great Blessings. But when bad things happened to them, they had to blame evil, Satan, Devil, or even Lucifer for what these entities had brought to them in the form of destruction and harm that befell them. (Article – Rebecca Denova 2021)

23

HUMAN POWERS AND ABILITIES

P eople from all over the world have reported encounters with mysterious beings. Most of the time, they appear to bring important messages or lend much-needed assistance, then vanish without a trace. Could they be angels or guardian angels, or can they be dimensional beings traveling through portals to visit their person of interest? Since all visitors from outside our earthly realm are considered extraterrestrials, you would have to consider multiple theories. Are they literally from Heaven, or are they the result of the interaction of our consciousness with a profoundly mysterious universe? However, you view these visits; these real-life experiences are worth our attention and research.

Some of the most fascinating and spiritually uplifting stories of the unexplained are those stories of people perceiving their visitors as miraculous. These strange visitors take the form of answered prayers and are interpreted as the actions of guardian angels. These events provide comfort, strengthen faith, and even save lives. As we discussed earlier, these strange visitors seem to visit people when needed most. Encounters with angels or extraterrestrial beings leave us with infinite possibilities to learn more about them and provide growth and transformation. Most times, the visits are unexpected and happen when you least expect these entities to show up in your presence. It doesn't matter if they are spiritual angels or UFOs that visit unannounced with extraterrestrial contact. The best way to call on angels or other types of visitors is to be present of mind, aware, and look around for the signs to learn to increase your consciousness (total awareness). Tune into these spiritual frequencies and send a mental message to invite visitation requests. Experience and act upon the signs you receive from angels or other entities. (Visitors/Real Angel Stories – Beliefnet)

The Powers and Abilities of Us Human Beings

Humans are created by God in His image and likeness and are the dominant species on Earth.

Human beings are living beings created by God after He made angels. Initially, when God created humans, He gave them a spiritual essence, also powerful energy that makes us humans unique. People's souls have tremendous power and purity. Still, after their expulsion from the (Garden of Eden), the heritability of humanity began to deteriorate until humans degraded to the state of weak and stupid creatures. They are infinitely far more vulnerable than their ancestor's spiritual power and longevity. It seems that because of this sinful act that Eve was tricked by the serpent (reptilian), both Adam and Eve were diminished to the lesser humans of power and spirituality that exist in us today. Before all these changes in the human spirit, we could seek out God more openly and call the angels for help anytime we needed God's help. Humans also started losing their longer life spans, like Noah and Enoch, that lived a thousand years. We humans today must relearn to connect with our spirituality and hope God hears us in our prayers. Ancient civilizations were more intelligent than modern-day humans. Scientists and scholars are rethinking the ancient peoples' intelligence and spirituality as they find more artifacts and text that prove most were highly sophisticated cultures. Did ancient extraterrestrials influence them? Most researchers think that ancient people were taught technology by aliens, like; building beautiful architectural buildings, medicine, abilities of telekinesis, moving large objects with sound frequencies, and taught them their inner abilities of spiritual power. (Humans/Supernatural Fanon Wiki/Fandom)

As this book suggests, the ancients practiced supernatural powers with some alien help to master their environment. Today, those powers are hidden from us by the world's elites and possibly by the aliens, in conjunction with human Leaders of government and higher elite religious figures. We are being told that humans are limited in our supernatural powers and lied to for thousands of years by history, which was written to hide our spiritual talents. Did you know that our soul and spirit are much larger than the physical body? And our soul is not limited or confined by the physical world? Our bodies can move through time and space, connecting us with other dimensions of reality and lifeforms that exist throughout creation—making us supernatural beings and presently dormant within our consciousness and spirits, forgetting how to release those supernatural abilities. This is due to our world and spiritual perception that has been watered down throughout history by the powers to be – not God. God is waiting for us to acknowledge the supernatural abilities he gave us in the beginning and use them for peace and love.

The first human beings are the masterpiece of the Most High, made in his image and likeness; they possessed tremendous power and purity that emanated a powerful Divine Light. The following is a list of those forgotten abilities of the first created human beings.

- **Divine body:** The first human beings, like Adam and Eve, had extremely powerful spirit bodies.
- **Immortality:** The first humans could live forever; they had an infinite life.
- **Intangibility:** The first humans can pass through any physical matter.

- **Supernatural perception:** The first humans can perceive the true face of all supernatural entities.
- **Teleportation:** Humans can teleport instantly to any place on Earth.
- **Omnilingualism:** They could understand and use non-verbal communication without prior language knowledge.
- **Advanced intelligence:** Humans can instantly analyze and understand anything like (social and technological) work and use their intelligence to build and produce early technologies that we are newly rediscovering.
- **Eidetic Memory:** Humans used to have total recall and permanently understand anything they saw or read. Their brains had an unlimited capacity for knowledge storage.

The Human Weaknesses

The forbidden fruit! When Adam and Eve ate the fruit of the knowledge of good and evil in the (Garden of Eden). The price of sin was spiritual condemnation, which led to the expulsion from the Garden of Eden. Supposedly, that is where we are today with limited supernatural abilities – but we can get them back through self-teaching our consciousness. (Humans/Supernatural Fanon Wiki/Fandom)

24

ACTUAL EXPERIENCES WITH
ANGELS OR EXTRATERRESTRIALS

IN THEIR WORDS

A Security Camera Captured an Angel

Michigan resident Glenn Thomas told (Inside Edition) an angel touched him after discovering his motion-sensor security camera captured an image of one hovering over his pickup truck. He instantly sent his photo to the pastor of his church, Danielle Moes, who then shared the photo on Facebook. Many locals believe the figure in the picture is a sign from Heaven. Moes' Facebook post has since obtained hundreds of shares. Pic (Guideposts)

An Angelic Nurse

Luke was diagnosed with bone cancer when he was just eight years old. A nurse came into Luke's hospital room during a two-week hospital stay required to treat an infection. As he slept, his mom spoke with the nurse, who was wearing a 1960s work uniform which she thought was strange. The nurse told Luke's mom she would pray for his healing before exiting.

Luke was fully healed of his infection and is now cancer free. According to (Thought Co.), both Luke and his mom believe the nurse, who was never seen again, was a guardian angel who offered them hope during a difficult time. The hospital staff and doctor said they did not have a nurse come into Luke's room during those hours. Author's note: Extraterrestrials have been known to shapeshift into humans that they copied, as in doppelganger duplication of a human being. (Guideposts)

Orbs in Photographs

I believed in angels all my life, especially in my younger years. I lived an exciting life, threw caution to the wind, and put myself in dangerous positions. I used to think I had worked my angels overtime.

My life changed when I saw orbs that showed up in photos I took at my son's wrestling tournament. I don't see things like these orbs that I saw in the pictures. I was upset! My middle and youngest sons both told me not to worry. They believed they were guardian angels. Since then, I have taken pictures of orbs in wonderful variations of colors. One had moth-like wings-gorgeous pink on top and a fairy green on the bottom. But when I am out with these orbs, I feel delighted. I found them playful and fun-loving, and they are a blessing to me. They have helped me with unreasonable fears. I have peace and serenity and see God's hand on everything now. Love and light go together. Ghost hunters also take pictures of orbs and see them as spirits moving about. Extraterrestrials use orbs as little drones to observe our human activities. (Penny) (Guideposts)

My brother Jan had his security cameras on and caught these orbs in his house. They would appear like bright balls of white light orbs (different round sizes). He thought it could be their dog that passed away several years ago. There were a lot more orbs than these pictures show. These pictures were taken in the last couple of years.

Bright, Beautiful Light

I've never experienced anything like this, but it was amazing. So, every night I will say a prayer, "Now I lay me down to sleep, I pray the Lord, my soul, to keep, guard me Jesus through the night and wake me with the morning light."

It happened to me. When I woke up, out of nowhere, I saw a beautiful bright light filling up my room. I thought somebody had turned on the light in the room, but I remembered my light was very dim. Then, I thought about my windows, but I always keep the blinds closed. I soon fell asleep with a great feeling and sense of security. When comparing this person's experience of bright light, extraterrestrial experiencers also see bright lights in their rooms and even entities in the room. The bright light is a sign of something entering the building. Brishauna (Guideposts)

Archangel Michael Visitation

I was giving a new client a reiki treatment. My hands were focused on her body, as were my eyes. Suddenly, I felt a presence in the room. When I lifted my head, I saw an angel step through the wall into the room. He was so tall that he had to stoop down not to bump his head on the ceiling. "Author's note, if the angel walked through the wall, why would he stoop to avoid the ceiling?" I thought he must be Archangel Michael because I had been told once that archangels are tall. I don't know why I thought it was Michael; I was just sure it was due to my first gut feeling.

I was unsure if I should tell the client about the angel visitation, so I kept quiet. Before the session ended, the woman asked if I had ever sensed angels. I quietly answered, "Yes," as I continued to look over at the beautiful being of light that was sending enormous amounts of love and caring into the room. The client then told me she had always felt a strong connection to the Archangel Michael. So, I told her he was in the room. It was an amazing experience. Maybe the client had an angel connection and enjoyed the peace and love a reiki session has on a body. Again, Tall White extraterrestrials also look like what this person described as tall and with a bright white light glow. (Paula) (Personal Stories of Angel Encounters)

Guardian Angel Encounters

At eighteen years of age, I was in a car wreck. A lady in white clothes appeared out of nowhere, like a nurse. She held a towel to my head, stopping my severe bleeding as the firetrucks came. She said, "You will be fine now." I looked away, and she was gone. I asked the fireman where the lady was, "What lady?" I pointed to where she had come from, and he said she could not have come from that area. That was a five-hundred-foot cliff to the Pacific Ocean.

Years later, I met her on the beach, and she said, "I heard about the accident and was at the beach and came to help you." All my friends saw her talk to me thirty years later. A blonde lady walked over to me and said, "You are going to be okay; everything will be fine." She walked away, and I turned around and realized it was her again, my guardian angel. (Mel S)

Angels in the Backyard

When I was taking pictures in my backyard one and a half years ago, I looked to see how the photos appeared. A great, awesome cloud came down my alley and three UFOs shaped like pyramids were in my backyard. Three men wearing silver suits and silver cone-shaped hats advanced from the UFOs toward me.

The one closest to me, about eight feet tall, had a great smile and reached out as if he was going to hug me. He looked as common as any man except for his silver suit. I overwhelmed with excitement and surprise. Unfortunately, being new to photography, the photos were lost when downloading them to the computer. The message error said that the space on the memory card was used up, so I could not transfer photos to it. This was highly frustrating. Nevertheless, the experience shores up other encounters with the Kingdom of God in various visions. This story of tall aliens Edgar met seemed like the tall white aliens reported in ancient and modern times. They appeared humanoid, like angels that can shapeshift into another body. (Edgar Ronnie Barton) (Beliefnet)

A Pastor in Need Meets a Stranger

Pastor John Boston was driving down the road when another car crossed the center line and came barreling toward him. The Pastor swerved to miss the vehicle and struck a utility pole, sending a live transformer crashing into his car. Immediately the metal and glass began to buckle from the intense heat from thousands of volts of electricity. His four-year-old daughter was with him and was trapped inside the burning car. The seat belt was stuck, and the door wouldn't open. That is when a scruffy looking stranger came out of nowhere and easily opened the smashed door. The man removed him from the car and walked him twenty feet away from the vehicle to safety before the car exploded in flames.

"He said my name is Johnny, the police are almost here, and I can't be here when they get here, but you're going to be okay," said Pastor Boston. "And then the man was gone."

He said that people who tried to rationalize the situation thought the circuit breaker tripped and Johnny fled because of a sketchy past. However, firefighters say some aspects of what happened defied logic, reason, and science. Pastor Boston was convinced he encountered an angel that day. This author needs clarification about what happened to the daughter. (Pastor John Boston) (Stories of Heavenly Visitors/ Real Angel Stories – Beliefnet)

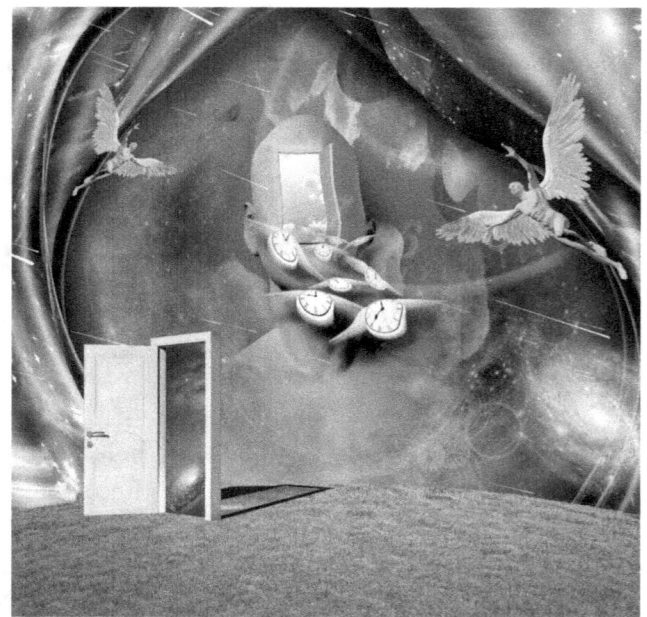

Soviet Cosmonauts in Space See Beings as Big as a Jet Airliner with Human Faces – True Story from 1984

In July 1984, Russian cosmonauts aboard the Soviet space station Salyut seven were on day one hundred fifty-five of their mission. On that day, the crew of six cosmonauts all saw the same strange lights and beings. According to commander Oleg Atkov and cosmonauts Vladimir Solovyov and Leoid Kizim, the space station was completely bathed in a mesmerizing orange light. The light appeared to enter from outside the space station and bled through an opaque wall. (ps://madmimi.com/s/b51b36) 9-29-22)

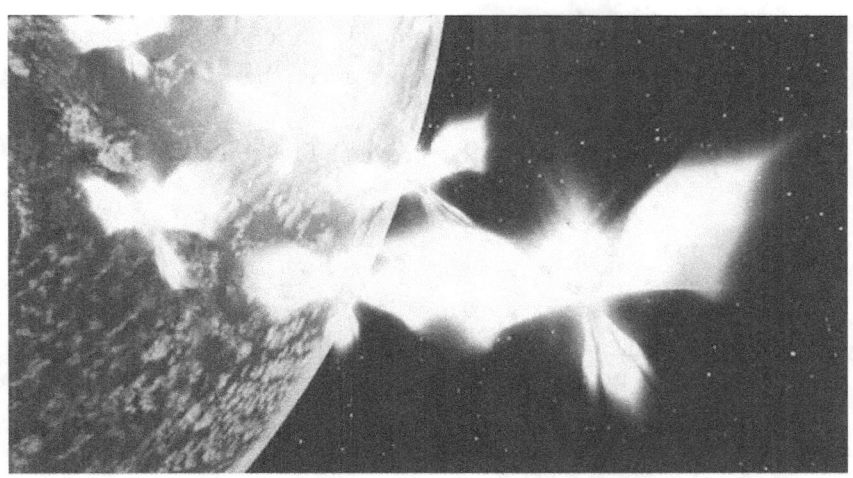

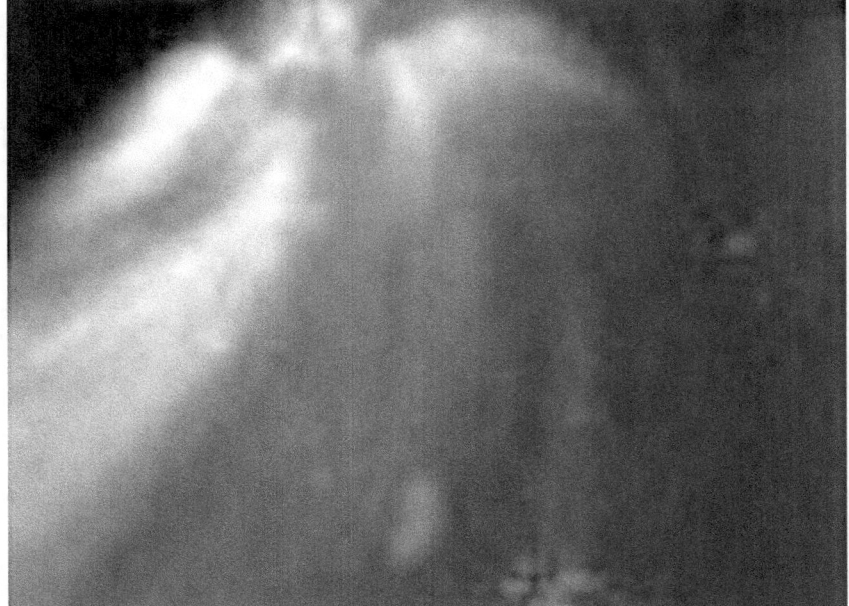

Orange Light

During that time, the crew witnessed the bright orange light; it was so bright that it blinded them temporarily. When their sight returned to normal, each of the six crew members looked out of the portholes for the source of the light, looking specifically for a possible explosion of their space station. From their experience, the Salyut seven had suffered previous fires. But what the crew saw was incomprehensible than the orange light, nothing like previous fires they had witnessed.

Second Appearance

On day one hundred sixty-seven, the crew was joined by another team of three from the T-12 spacecraft: Svetlana Savitskaya, Igor Volk, and Vladimir Dzhanibekov. Right after this, other crew members joined the main group of cosmonauts once again; they were bathed in warm orange light. Then, like the first time this happened with the strange orange light, they immediately looked out from the portholes and saw these angelic beings again. According to the cosmonauts, these beings were reported as the size of an "airliner," with large heads. Of course, this event was deemed top secret by the Soviet Union, and the crew was cautioned not to speak of this event publicly.

All the cosmonauts reported seeing the faces of seven angels hovering outside their space station. They called down to ground control and told them they were humanoid in appearance (faces and bodies looked human), but they had wings and halos. These angelic beings kept pace with their space station for ten minutes before vanishing.

The authentic video footage was released by a Russian Whistleblower, providing tons of essential information that the Illuminati has known about for a long time. This Whistleblower spoke the truth and confirmed many concerning planetary shifts as we enter a new dimension and frequency. This group of cosmonauts seeing these giant angels proved that spiritual warfare is real. It has been a long and ongoing battle between the EVILS, aka "Illuminati," that have infiltrated and conquered our planet, and the good ones currently at war with one another. The elites and the Illuminati designed this information that has been kept from the public to keep their secrets to themselves for control of the world. These secretive groups have known for many years that there were Good and Bad battles around our planet, angels VS evil.

This article was rewritten this year, 2022, and the writer feels a need to share this information about the Illuminati and the battles of Good VS Evil around our planet. These events are happening right now, this writer says, right within our own Earth space. This author knows nothing of the Illuminati responsible for this cover-up of these Good VS Evil battles. The public has never even discussed this story since 1984 in an open media sense. This author needs to prove this part of the story. Can it be true? Yes, anything can happen during these tumultuous modern times. (ps://madmimi.com/s/b51b36)

25

PERSONAL AND FAMILY SIGHTINGS OF REAL ANGELS

MY MOTHER, STELLA EMMONS,' ANGELIC RESCUE

It was May 29th, 1968; my mom was trying to give birth to twins at the age of forty-two and started developing bleeding problems. Her doctor was summoned to her room at the Hospital in Alton, Illinois, but he had to travel by car to get to her location. The nurses were assisted by another doctor (not an Obstetrician) to help keep her heart and breathing functioning normally. My mother passed out and didn't remember anything after that. She heard the nurses keep saying, "Hang in there, Mrs. Emmons, the doctor, is coming soon. My mother was coming in and out of consciousness, but she could understand the medical staff being very concerned about her medical emergency.

My Dad arrived soon after my mom went out of consciousness. The medical staff said my mom's life was in a severe medical condition. My dad told the medical staff that he needed to call his two sons at the Army boot camp at Fort Leonard Wood in Missouri to take us home. Of course, one of those sons was me, and the other was my brother Jack. The medical staff called the Red Cross to contact the Army to get us home on an emergency pass. It all happened very fast that the Red Cross contacted the Army, and we were on a bus on our way home on a four-hour drive to the hospital.

During that time, my mom was unconscious while waiting for the doctor to do surgery on her. She said she had very pleasant dreams while unconscious about floating and seeing clouds wisping by her. She was heading towards a tunnel of white light. Then she heard the nurse say your sister Virginia is calling, and for some reason, she came out of the unconscious state. My mother said her sister Virginia never calls her. She took this as a sign that her sister was being used as an angel to keep my mother alive. At that same moment, the doctor was performing surgery to give more room for the babies to pass through the birth canal. The doctor brought both babies out and completed the birthing procedure. Then the doctor attended to my mom's bleeding problems in time before she bled out. We could not see my mother due to her weakness, but we waited outside her room. The sad part is that my mom and family lost a baby daughter/sister because she was born with an enlarged head and brain damage. She passed the next day, and only my dad could see her. My mom was fine the next day, and my brother and I had to return to the Army. God and His angels blessed us.

My Sister Met an Angel by Her Hospital Bed

In May 2022, my sister Sherry had an unusual encounter in her hospital room while waiting for triple bypass heart surgery later that morning. It was around 3 am when my sister said she felt a presence come into the room. She was awake and conscious of what she was witnessing at the time of the angel's visit. She said she knew when the hospital staff would walk into her room because the large entrance door would flood the room with light from the nurses' desk and hall-way. She did not know it was a strange visit from an angel until she approached her by her bedside. My sister said she did not see the large door open, and no light flooded her room.

My sister has very intuitive, almost psychic abilities and can attract people who have messages for her in her dreams that have passed away—kind of an empathic person. She noticed someone approaching her and got within a couple of feet of her bed. My sister looked at her and said there was enough light to see the lady. She said she had strange feelings of elation going through her body, like energy that this lady was giving off. They both looked each other in the eyes, and the lady asked, "are you all right?" My sister said yes, I am fine, just a little nervous about the heart surgery later this morning. The lady said, "you will be fine, don't worry." My sister then watched the lady leave the room but said she did not see her open the door to her room because no light came through the door from the hallway.

My sister then turned over in bed and drifted off to sleep, wondering to whom that person was giving her kind words. She said the lady was about five feet five inches tall and dressed in loose dark-colored dress slacks with a light purple loose top – civilian clothes, not medical. This strange lady had a short, cropped "bobbed" haircut and light blonde hair and was slightly overweight. My sister said she was in her mid-fifties and had a very soft-toned voice. After the lady left her room, she felt it strange for a woman in civilian clothes to enter her room at 3 am.

The next day my sister Sherry spoke with the hospital staff and asked who that lady was that came into her room at 3 am. They looked at her and said, nobody was authorized to be in your room at that time of morning without nurses' uniforms or ID. Then they ran an acuity test on her to see if my sister was all right and not hallucinating. Their test turned up negative for any lapses of mental acuity. The medical staff was perplexed about the visit. So, my sister feels like it was an angel visit. I spoke to her a day after her successful heart surgery, and the visitor (angel) was correct. My sister recovered very well.

My Brother Jay saw Angels Floating over His Bed

When our father passed away in 1995, my brother Jay was distraught at his passing. He could not sleep very well that night. Predictably, none of the family could sleep well after a death in the family.

My brother said he felt suddenly comforted in bed that night. He then saw a white light scattered throughout the bedroom like a moving, pulsing light. He said he was conscious and awake during this strange event. He shared a room with another brother but did not witness this event. My brother Jay did.

As he explains it, the light turned into several flying angels, and they were small, about six inches in length, and with six-inch wings. He said they were pure white and shining with a glittering effect. Jay said he saw six hovering angels over him in bed just inches away. After about fifteen seconds, he said they all disappeared, leaving him with awe and a warm spiritual feeling. He felt our father was telling him he was all right and happy now. So, after my brother's experience with these angels, he felt more self-assured about his grief and worry, giving him peace. Jay drew these pictures of the angels he saw on paper.

My Own Personal Angel Visitations

My first angel sighting was in 1971; this happened at my parents' house in Illinois after my military duty. I shared a bedroom with two other brothers briefly before I got my apartment. I felt strange a little before this event happened. You know that feeling of being jittery and beside yourself with your emotions. For some unknown reason, I felt an energy or a presence near me, like somebody was watching me. This happened around 3 am in the middle of the night. The bewitching hour is when all paranormal or spiritual events happen.

I was wide awake when I saw this "Lady in White." She was standing at the foot of my bed, looking at me with peace and serenity. I was shocked and very much surprised at the sight of this Lady. She was about five foot eight inches tall; she had her head covered with a thin white veil, so I could not see her face or hair. It was a female figure, not a man in a robe. The pure white robe was long and covered her whole body and was ruffled like a wedding gown with pleats. We both stared at each other for around ten seconds while I was leaning on my right elbow to get a good look. Then, very slowly, she turned and walked away very gracefully.

The "Lady in White" walked across the hallway, and I could see her very well because the bedroom door was wide open. She was heading to my mom and dad's bedroom, and I saw her turn to where my mother slept. I got up immediately and followed the lady into my mom's bedroom, where she was sleeping. I went into their room and asked my mom if she had seen the "Lady in White?" She said no, and I asked her if she was all right, and my mom said yes, of course. I told her what I saw, and my mom said you saw an angel, and I hope that means good blessings.

My Second Lady in White Visitation

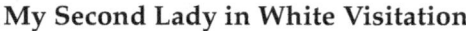

Some years later, in 1999, in a house just four houses down from my mother's house that I bought in 1993. I had another visit by this angel in white. Angels are attracted to people in distress, as I was at my mother's house just after Vietnam combat duty in 1971. That is when I saw my first Lady in White. This time I was in some stressful changes during a divorce and after my ex-wife moved out. I imagine that brought this angel back to show herself to me again. She felt my life change, so the angel wanted to lift my spirits.

While in my bed in Godfrey, Illinois, again, it was 3 am mid-morning when the Lady in White made her appearance to me. Like the last visit in 1971, I felt some strange energy vibrating around my body. I sat up in bed and looked at the foot of my bed, and there she was, standing very quietly with a veil over her head in the same long pleated white (wedding gown) style of a robe. She stood there for ten seconds, looking at me. Then turned and started walking to my bath-room just off my bedroom area. She walked at the same slow pace, very elegantly. I got up and followed her into my bathroom, but she disappeared quickly. It was the same long pleated robe and thin veil over her head. I could not see her face. Yes, I felt in awe of this spiri-tual moment happening again. Still, I don't know if the lady was an angel or an extraterrestrial.

My Experience with an Old Cowboy Angel

This experience occurred in October of 2010 in Sedona, Arizona, on the front porch of the Lodge I was staying at. I met with an extraterrestrial that same day that I wrote about in my first book, "They," What do they want? It was around 4 pm, and light rain was falling, and it was cool. Since Sedona is only pretty when it is not raining, I decided to leave. However, I heard weather reports before I started going. Arizona had its first tornado warnings in fifty years that day I was departing. I heard the weatherperson say the tornado warnings were for Northwest of Flagstaff, just thirty minutes North of Sedona.

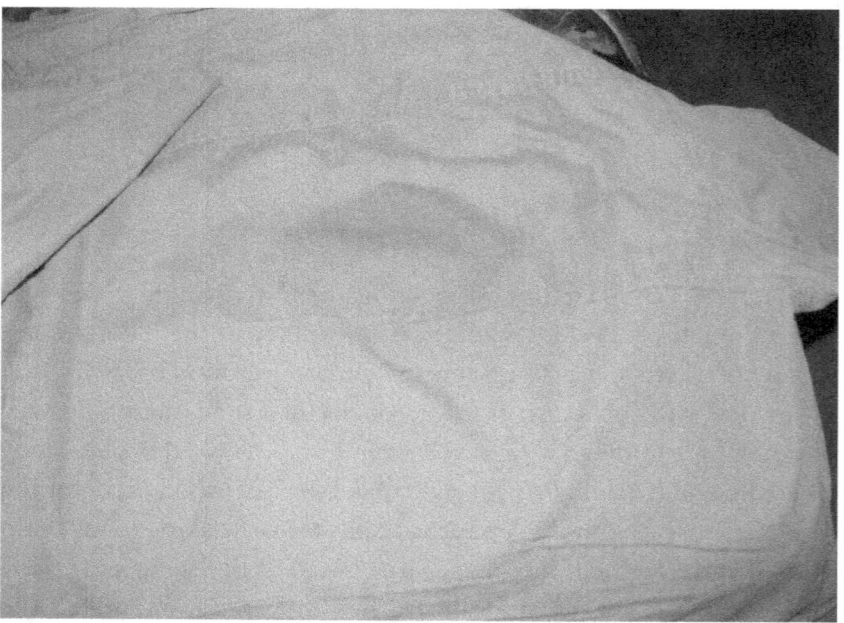

I was loading my car with my luggage and checking out of my room. It was drizzling, so I was in a hurry. Suddenly, I hear the voice of an older gentleman saying, "Mister, are you leaving now?" I look up, and I see this old Guy dressed in suspenders, an old dirty plaid design shirt, old dirty denim jeans, and a cowboy hat that was well used; he looked to be seventy years old and was rocking in a rocking chair while talking to me. He also had worn-out brown cowboy boots but wore a gentle smile on his face that had long whiskers. I told him I was leaving Sedona because it was raining. He said, "I wouldn't leave if I were you." Then he pointed up to the clouds rolling in that looked omnibus. Again, he said, "I would not leave now." I said the bad weather would not be east of us. That is my direction of travel. He again said, "do not leave." Well, I drove off to the North towards Flagstaff.

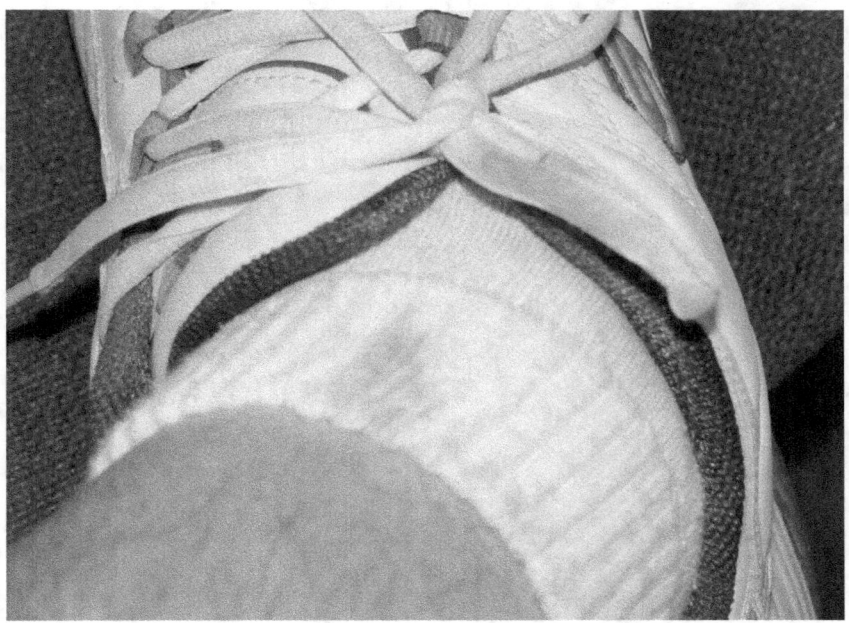

When I got to Interstate forty-four, it started to hail lightly and rain more. As I kept traveling East toward New Mexico, the weather got worse. The hail increased in size, about the size of tennis balls. I looked up and saw a vast rotating scary tornado cloud twirling black and ugly ready to touch down. The large hail I thought would break my windshield out. For thirty minutes, I traveled with this weather front and had to slow down because of a lack of visibility. I knew the car was taking a pounding because I could see the tennis ball size hail hit the water puddles and create a large splash. Finally, I got to the

New Mexico border, and the weather cleared up. I looked at my car, and there was hail damage ($2,500.00 worth). My old Guy, my guardian angel, was correct; he tried to warn me, but I did not heed his warning. Let that be a lesson; always listen to advice, especially if it strangely comes to you. There were no rocking chairs on the Lodge's porch, only log benches – my missed sign.

Angel Helped me at Angel Rock, New Mexico

Strange things do happen, like accidents we are not prepared for. This angel incident occurred in 2011 during the summer months in New Mexico. This incident happened about twenty miles Southwest of Gallup, New Mexico, near the Hopi Reservation. A small Café and a Gift Shop were at the bottom of Angel Rock. Angel Rock was a single-standing small Butte that was red and gray rock and very pretty. Hence the name Angel Rock. I wanted to take pictures of the Rock and visit the gift shop. Simple enough?

After securing my coffee mug in the car's cup holder console, I got out of my car. It was around 9 am when I arrived at the Angel Rock location. After I set everything up in my car, I got out of the car to take pictures with my camera of Angel Rock. Seconds after I started taking the pictures, my car started rolling slowly and turned to the left by itself. I turned to look at my car after I noticed the movement of my car and heard the gravel make noises. Sure, I panicked and threw my camera in the car seat, then I tried to jump in my vehicle while it was slowly rolling. After throwing my camera in the car, I started to jump in the car to take control. At that very moment, the car sped up much faster when I leaped into the seat. Well, I came up short because of the increased speed of the vehicle, which caused me to lose balance. I hung on the car by the door handle, thinking I could slow the vehicle down. That was a wrong plan because I fell face down on the gravel lot after dragging about fifteen feet hanging on the door.

While on the ground, I watched the car roll past me; at least, that is what I thought. I was very close to the back tire because I could smell the tire rubber when it passed me. When I got off the ground, I watched my car roll across an embankment and a two-lane road ending up in a ditch near a fence on the other side of the road. At that moment of standing up, a Lady came over to me and asked if I was all right and that she would call an ambulance. I said I was fine, but my left leg had a bad gravel rash and bleeding. The Lady said, oh no, your back tire ran over your foot and your right shoulder; I saw it, she said. Look at the back of your shirt; it has black rubber marks. I said I don't feel any pain in my shoulder or foot. Just my scratched-up left leg.

The Lady kept watching me and said I should not be standing. I was more worried about my car at that time.

The Lady said, "I hope you are all right." She stayed with me until I got help. At the time of the accident, I saw a Native American Native man walking out of the café carrying a pan and dumping it on the ground. He just stared at me during the whole incident – I found that odd. Then, my angelic humans came out of their shop to assist me and medically treat my leg. The woman was an ex-nurse, so she took me to her shop and cleaned up my left leg. Her husband went to my car, which was in the embankment off the road. He could not get in the car because it was locked. So, I called OnStar to unlock the car, and he retrieved my car for me. The nurse lady told me to look at my shirt because it had tire treads on the right shoulder.

I took off the shirt to look at the back of it, and sure enough, there were tire treads on the right shoulder. Also, we found tire treads on my right foot in the white sock area. They were charming people and can be said to be human angels. I felt all right, except the left leg was torn up by gravel but not bad enough to go to the hospital. I took care of it myself after the nurse told me what to do. I have pictures of the sock and my shirt with tire treads. I called my insurance company immediately and said I had had an accident. They said, "are you all right?" I said yes, but my pride was hurt because my car ran over me. There were scratches on my car from the fence but not very much damage.

I feel my Guardian Angel helped pick up the car's weight off me so as not to cause me much bodily harm. That is what I told my angelic human newly founded friends. They agreed that I should have been badly injured by looking at my clothing, and the Lady that witnessed the car rolling over me told the shop owners that the car rolled over me before she left. Synchronicity? Being at Angel Rock and being helped by a supernatural angel and human angels.

26

SIGNS THAT GHOSTS OR SPIRITS HAVE VISITED YOU

Before we get started with the signs that ghosts or spirits might have visited you, we need to understand the types of energy you might encounter. Of course, this would include ghosts, spirits, angels, demons, fairies, residuals, extraterrestrials, and elementals. Elementals are spirits that reside on the astral plane just above our atmosphere. These spirits use sorcery to control our sphere of existence. They protect all living creatures and act as guardians that protect us from evil. Ghosts are identified as Spirits that have not crossed over into Heaven, whereas spirits are often used to classify those who have crossed over into the "light."

There are some key differences between encountering a Ghost and a Spirit that will help you identify your experience.

Spirits will usually make you feel peaceful and calm, comforted and reassured. Spirits can often enter your dreams and communicate through sometimes very vivid pictures and words as a message of sorts. This could be a past relative or someone you recently met, appearing as an apparition; either way, the feeling surrounding a spirit is often a calm and pleasant experience. Most dreams you won't remember, but a lucid or vivid dream you won't forget. They appear very real, with an easy-to-understand message about who or what they are telling you.

On the other hand, ghosts often leave you with an eerie horror movie feeling, making you uncomfortable sometimes. These ghostly figures can appear as apparitions, shadows, orbs, or ectoplasm mist. They may also attach to an object or living person – ask Ghost Investigators; they can tell you some scary stories of ghosts following them home. In my experiences with extraterrestrials, these same observations that ghosts and spirits elicit can also be characteristics of ETs. They are invisible, invade your dreams, move objects, touch you, and show themselves as shadow beings.

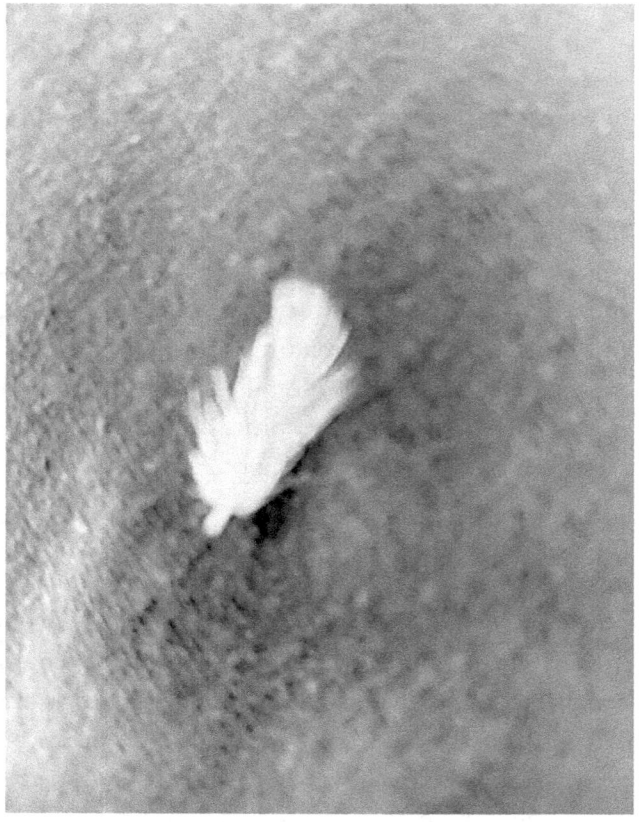

Common Signs that you have a Visitor from the other side

- **Unexplained noises:** Hearing sounds such as footsteps, knocking, banging, scratching, or something being dropped.
- **Opening door/cupboards:** Any doors or cupboards that seem to open independently without explanation.
- **Lights switching on and off:** Having lights come on or turn off without you flipping the switches or light bulbs that seem to blow out quickly.
- **Electronics switching on and off:** Items like televisions or radios switching on/off or changing channels and increased static or increasing volume. Sometimes you might be thinking of a loved one, and their favorite song starts playing. These and other mentioned signs, especially the television changing channels I am experiencing now. Paranormal activities sometimes follow extraterrestrial visits – I have experienced that also. (Tanaaz – Conscious Forever)
- **Shadows:** Seeing unexplained shadows in the corner of your eyes.
- **Disappearing items:** An everyday item that suddenly vanishes from its usual spot, only to see it reappear a few days later. Not to be joking, but this has caused arguments between wives and husbands looking for these items. A playful ghost or entity?
- **Feelings of being watched:** This is common among most of us. This feeling can be eerie. However, it doesn't necessarily mean the presence itself is negative energy.
- **Hot and cold spots:** substantial temperature fluctuations in particular areas of your home.
- Feelings of being touched: If you ever felt somebody or something brush past, a poke, push, or nudge. A harmful energy touching you that leaves scratches could be an evil spirit.

- **Unexplained smells:** Fragrances not in your house that leave a foul odor are usually from a negative presence.
- **Cries/Whispers/Voices:** Hearing soft chatter, cries, whispers, or even music from an unknown source when it is quiet usually could be a visitor.
- **Levitating Objects:** If this happens, this could be the most prominent characteristic that energy is present that could be either evil or good.
- **Apparitions:** Seeing human-formed apparitions or entities can be a misty cloud-like fog and transparent or solid entities.
- **Orbs:** If you see brightly colored orbs – blue orbs are often spirits, and white orbs are often Angels. Orbs, from my experience, are around extraterrestrials when they enter your domain. They are usually white orbs that float about and are more easily caught by cameras. The human eye cannot see orbs at the frequencies they exist most of the time.
- **Objects at your feet:** Seeing coins, stones, and feathers at your feet or even in your clothing could have been sent by a loved one or spirit. Apports, as the Ufologist may call them – are any item that mysteriously shows up without an explanation. (Signs a Ghost or Spirit is visiting You – Forever Conscious) (Tanaaz)
- **Animal Sensitivities:** Your pets will likely sense a spiritual or energy presence before humans do. Dogs can sense magnetic and electrical fields because their eyes have a light-detecting protein called cryptochrome. A dog and cat have one hundred thousand times more powerful sense of smell than us humans. A cat has a more powerful sense of smell, touch, and vision, but that does not mean cats have a sixth sense – they don't.
- **Residuals:** Residuals are an imprint of energy that seems to be caught on a continuous loop and playing repeatedly. Some believe residual energy can be cleared by sage and

other smudging rituals, incense, and crystals. This author has never seen these clearing rituals ever really work. Your mind and spirit can clean these residual spirits with God's help. So, if you hear bumps and noises in the night, it may not be ghosts but residual energies. If you are experiencing paranormal activity in your home, take a few moments to observe the energy you feel, be calm in your emotions, and create a positive energy instead of a fearful feeling. The spiritual energy you feel could be a loved one coming back to visit. (Forever Conscious – Tanaaz)

27

SIGNS YOU'RE BEING VISITED BY YOUR GUARDIAN ANGEL

Guardian Angels know that humans are skeptical and that we often question our sixth sense and intuition (Gut feelings); the angels will send us messages perceptible through scent. Most of the time, it is an unexpectedly pleasant smell. This could be that a guardian angel is nearby. Have you ever smelled a perfume you are familiar with? Or, had a sense of smelling roses or lavender flowers in your house when the flowers were not in your home? These sweet smells could be a sign/message that you have an angel visiting you. People have smelled the pleasant fragrance of perfume or aftershave of a past loved one in their surroundings, even at work.

Angels will also send messages through sight and sound. Seeing angel shapes in clouds could be a phenomenon researchers call pareidolia which is a false perception. It is like the mind sees what it wants to see. But then again, it is in the eyes of the beholder and what it means to them. If a person feels like it is an angel's message, then they should go by their feelings and intuition. A ringing in your ears could be a message sent by angels and may sound different than tinnitus. For me, it has been a tapping sound on the eardrum or short beeps like a telegraph tapping out letters. (Signs Your Guardian Angel is Near – Beliefnet)

Angels will use music and songs to convey messages in several ways. The lyrics of a song could have significant meaning to a person that will elicit feelings of memories with loved ones. It could reaffirm your intuition, or a song might lift your spirits and reassure you that everything is fine. When a song you were thinking about suddenly plays on the radio or television, that could mean your guardian angel is communicating with you through music. This could be an old song that brings about fond memories you have not heard for a long time, but it especially touches you or sends you the very message you needed at that moment. We call that synchronicity that nothing happens by accident and occurs at the right moment.

Angels will leave objects at your feet to get your attention and send a message. A white feather is the most common article that angels leave for a message from a loved one. Most of the time, these objects, like feathers, are put across your path in an extremely unlikely location. Small toys, rocks, and coins are popular with angels, but odd trinkets are also found in a person's path. This is a message from your guardian angel to help guide you in the right direction or send a message which is usually the first thought that comes to your mind and heart. This author has had small white feathers laid at my feet several times. Once, at my dear brother's funeral, he died too young. About five feet from his casket, the feather was laid at my left foot, only inches away. Angels and spiritual energies work in supernatural ways. On this occasion, near my brother Mick's casket was my brother saying he was fine, and it was all right, brother.

Angels use repetition, or you witness specific names or locations repeated by several people or by radio and TV that draw your curiosity. Guardian angels use humor to help you take notice by repeating specific phrases or words – repetition. Take, for instance, a person. Within a matter of days, three different people mention the same person. This might be a sign to get in touch with this person. The angels don't give up on you. If you hear the same thing repeatedly, listen and act upon it. If you experience repeated coincidences, synchronicities, or dreams around the same theme, pay attention because your guardian angel may be trying to tell you something important. If you feel strongly that something is a message of guidance from your guardian angel, it likely is. Angels are simple and do not necessarily make grand gestures when sending messages; they use what's available and are part of our daily lives. Like Jesus, He spoke in parables to help the people of that era understand what he was saying since education was limited in those days. Like angels, they won't get too technical with their supernatural abilities in communicating with us because we may not understand their message.

The Bible tells us, "Beware that you don't look down on any of these little ones. For I tell you that in Heaven, their angels are always in the presence of my Heavenly Father" (Matthew 18:10). This is one of the key passages in the Bible regarding guardian angels. From scripture, we know that the role of guardian angels is to guard humans, institutions, cities, and nations. That is not the total duty of angels. Guardian angels exist, above all, to help us in spiritual difficulties. God is with us through the action of the angels, and they participate in our struggles to help us fulfill our calling. Life is full of struggles and dangers, both material and spiritual. Because of this, our divine Creator has placed an angel to watch over each one of us. (Signs Your Guardian Angel is Near – Beliefnet)

The Spiritual Meaning of Light in Angels and Miracles

Angels often appear as beings of light and use light's electromagnetic energy when traveling to and from Earth and Heaven. Electromagnetic energy replaces the wings concept that most people might see attached to an angel. When traveling through the different levels of dimensions, the energy propels them through dimensional walls or veils. Angels that were written earlier don't have wings; it is what they show humans who want them to have wings to comfort a human into believing they are seeing what they want to see. Angels, as we said earlier, are shapeshifters to appear to humans in a way that will comfort them and not alarm them. Miraculous events, such as apparitions, often feature light appearing in supernatural ways. Extraterrestrials also have bright white lights that witnesses have reported. White light, like the sun, has always been known to give life and lift the spirit of humans, plants, and animals. White light is also seen as a cleansing of the soul and is felt to have healing properties. Have you ever heard your parents tell you to go out and get some sun as a child?

Light is a Symbol of Life and Love

Light plays a huge role in the creation story, or as some researchers say, life was created by the "Big Bang." Most creation theories say that God created light before anything else. An example is the Bible famously records in (Genesis 1:3) that on the first day of creation: "God said, 'Let there be light,' and there was light." When God created light, energy from the light fueled life on our planet. Our ecosystem depends on light from the sun. To add to this thought, there are many suns in our universe, so could that energy also create life on other star systems? For example, plants use sunlight to make food in their leaves, while animals and people higher up the food chain get energy from the plants.

Spiritually, light is a symbol of life that comes from a loving creator who cares for creation. Just as all living things on Earth need sunlight to grow physically, people need the light of loving relationships with the creator – God, to grow spiritually and put love in our hearts. (Light in Angels and Miracles – Whitney Hopler)

Saint Francis of Assisi, the patron saint of animals who is famous for his reverence for all of creation, wrote a prayer praising God for the sun and its light: "Praise be to God for all His creatures, and especially our brother the sun who brings us the day and brings us the light. How beautiful He is! How splendid! Oh, He reminds us of you." But unfortunately, many ancient cultures, like the Egyptians, Mayans, and Greeks, worshipped the sun instead of God. Guess they were close to worshipping the sun, but they missed worshipping the real creator, God.

Muslims believe angels are made of light, a bright white pure light. A light that is loving with pure love from God. Angels are God's messengers; angels constantly deliver God's messages of loving encouragement to people. The light appearing during a miracle often indicates that God is at work in the situation, lovingly caring for the people. He is a blessing in a miraculous way (such as answering prayers in specific ways that would not be possible without His intervention). Miraculous apparitions also use light and may feature spectacular, supernatural light effects. Stories from people involved in supernatural events, like healing or angel visitations, always involve bright white light. Likewise, the bright white light that is seen in a tunnel with a near-death experience.

A Symbol of Wisdom

Light is often associated with wisdom. That is why we use the word "enlighten" to give someone knowledge or understanding (especially with spiritual insights). You have heard people say, "light bulb" just turned on in my head when new creative ideas inspire them. That is when they gained a better perspective or conclusion to their problem or situation, and they say, I looked at it "in a new light." In Spirituality, light stands for truth from the good side of the spiritual realm overcoming lies and the evil side of the opposite spiritual realm.

People with the spiritual enlightenment gift have the wisdom to choose the right path or truth over deception in their everyday lives.

People that have used meditation as a tool for prayer usually use candlelight or crystals to enhance their experience, and they both have to do with light. When communicating with angels, angels radiate electromagnetic energy just as light does. Angels also respond to a system of colors, corresponding to different colored light rays in the electromagnetic spectrum. These other colors will match certain angels' energy vibrations at specific frequencies to the light rays with similar frequencies. People seeking wisdom and help from angels about different issues and problems use colors and light to connect with angels specializing in different missions. One ray, red, focuses the most on wisdom, leading to Uriel, the Archangel of wisdom.

The world's major religious texts use light as a symbol of wisdom, and it encourages readers to develop closer relationships with God. God will light their spiritual paths through the darkness of a fallen, sinful world. Just as one looks into a mirror to see themselves, faithful people can engage in spiritual reflection to see the state of their souls. This reflection will motivate them to seek more spiritual wisdom. The process God uses to give people wisdom that seeks it is miraculous since this wisdom will make profound changes in the betterment of a person that receives God's wisdom. (www.learnreligions.com/spiritual-meaning-of-light-angels-miracles-124703)

A Symbol of Hope

Light is also a spiritual symbol of hope. In many religions, Light is considered salvation from the darkness of sin. Believers gain confidence knowing that letting their light of faith shine in a dark world can bring about fundamental positive changes for the betterment of their lives. The faithful will often light candles when praying for hope to create change in hopeless situations. The darkness is scary to humans because we lose a good portion of our visibility and clarity. That may be why Holly wood films movies in the dark, scary movies, especially to invoke darkness as the evil bringer of danger.

Major religious holidays use light to celebrate the power of spiritual hope. The usage of lights can be seen mainly at Christmas celebrations. Christians decorate with electric lights to symbolize Jesus Christ as the light of the world, our savior. The Hindus celebrate the hope of spiritual victories through fireworks and candles. The Jewish holiday of Hanukkah celebrates the hope that the Jewish people derived from the ancient Hanukkah miracle of lights. We, humans, are more joyous with light celebrations like fireworks and pretty lights in abundance. It makes us more energetic and happier deep within our souls. Humans are also more uplifted outdoors in the sunlight, like at the beach; we get stress release. Light is God!

Light can overpower darkness in the physical realm since the photons in light can dispel darkness, but darkness cannot. You can see where light dispels darkness by simply walking in a room with a flashlight. Light of any intensity can be seen in complete darkness, even a tiny candle in a pitch-black room or on a moonless night outside. This same principle applies spiritually, as the light of hope is always stronger than the darkness of discouragement and hopelessness. God often assigns angels to work on missions of hope that help people in need, and the results may be miraculous. It does not matter how bad a person's circumstances get; God can change those perilous times into a shining light of hope in one's life. (www.learnreligions. com/spiritual-meaning-of-light-angels)

28

HUMANS ARE SUPERNATURAL BEINGS

This might surprise you, but you are a supernatural being. All humans are equipped with a soul and a spiritual power that makes them supernatural. We can do magical things even if we are physical beings on the outside. This is because we have abundant spiritual energy inside our hearts and minds that exist throughout our whole body.

Who is a Supernatural Being?

A supernatural being is above or beyond natural. This would be a person who performs extraordinary things or miracles. We are all magical beings when we can channel our positive spiritual energies toward our dark feelings and hopelessness to use our light against darkness. When you start seeing yourself as an ordinary person, that is the perspective you will have about yourself. You will remain a lackluster negative soul until you see yourself as a spiritually positive person. Conversely, if you see yourself as a supernatural being, you will begin functioning in that capacity. If you still doubt that you are a supernatural being, the following reasons will make you know you are a supernatural being.

Inspiration

If you can get inspiration to do new things, that will show that there is something special about you. Everybody gets inspiration to do things from time to time, but if you say, "you've never gotten the inspiration to do anything," something is wrong. It is the inspiration that brings about inventions and the development of new technologies. Think of Einstein, Ford, Tesla, and Edison when you think about people with inspiration and hard work. As the world's people keep developing and coming up with new inventions, that is happening because inspiration is always available to bring new ideas into the light. Inspiration, like consciousness, comes to those that open their minds up to get knowledge. Inspiration will turn away from those that have a wrapped or closed mind. Everyone can get inspiration to be innovative and inventive if they open their minds. That goes to show that we are supernatural beings. It would appear we are saying that God and his angels plant inspiration and hope into a person's consciousness. (We are A Supernatural Being)

Creativity

Just like inspiration, every human on Earth can be creative. It is left to each person to seek and use their creative expressions for the good of all creation on Earth. Creativity is the ability to devise solutions to a problem or think through trouble. You have heard the old saying, "think outside the box," when all options seem to be exhausted. Inspiration can push you to draw a picture, but creativity helps you to draw the picture and paint it nicely from your spiritual powers. Both human strengths, inspiration, and creativity show the spiritual side of life. If you get next to God through meditation and deep prayer, your spirituality will grow, and your knowledge gathering will open widely.

Vision

Vision is not just seeing visually with your eyes; instead, it means the ability to see farther than where you are now in supernatural thought. The world is led by people with a talent for vision (who can see into the future) and make decisions based on their perceptions of the future. As humans, we can see visions; how far we go in life is a function of how far we can see into the future. Do not limit yourself to seeing small visions of your future but instead see big visions and succeed in life. In the spiritual aspect of one's being, what you see in life is what you get. If a person allows themselves to fail and does not utilize their spiritual attributes to overcome diversity, they will be a failure. Many people visualize different ideas, which is why we achieve other goals. A strong vision in your life is an essential aspect of life, and it can determine the course of your life in success or failure.

You Can Communicate with God

One of the facts about a supernatural person is that we all can pray to God. God never appears to us physically, but he is with us in spirit to communicate through our silence. We all have seen the power of prayer; it's a miracle for us and notices its effect on our lives. If we listen, it instills focus, and the whispers from God will lead us down the right path. We can pray to God and get a supernatural response in dark times. Pray to God regularly to maintain your spiritual health, and you will be amazed at how well God helps those who reach out to him. When confusion takes our lives, you can talk to God, and He will speak to you directly on how you should go.

Your Dreams Can Guide You

The other characteristic that shows you are a supernatural being is that we all can dream while we sleep. Or daydream, but that is less effective because there are interruptions. Sometimes our dreams are seemingly very real; we can see what will happen in the future. With this ability, we can go beyond human comprehension, which points to the fact that we are supernatural beings. Dreaming is not a natural thing we do for no reason at all. We dream because it is one means through which God communicates with us. You will also notice that you won't understand some of your dreams, but some people can interpret and understand your dreams. This is also a characteristic of a supernatural spiritual aspect of life. Not everybody can interpret dreams; not everyone can dream about the future. Whether we know it or not, we all dream, and people do not understand what they have dreamed about.

It would be best if you always realized you are first a spiritual being and then a physical being. That means you are a spiritual being experiencing life in the physical body form. Understanding that you are a supernatural being will help you perform exploits and abilities you never knew you could achieve. If you want to go high, you need to tap into that supernatural dimension that God has given you access to. (You Are a Supernatural Being)

CONCLUSION

I have always been fascinated by the supernatural world, even as a child playing with toys of supernatural heroes in the movies. My favorite scary movies are old movies like the invisible man and aliens from Mars. Later, as a teenager, I saw flying saucers in real life. So, I started knowing that aliens were real. I devoted a chapter in this book discussing extraterrestrials as being like angels because angels come from outside our realm. They can be invisible, shapeshift, read our minds, and know what we need in our darkest hours. I try not to put extraterrestrials on the same spiritual level as angels but discuss their similarities.

Do I believe in angels? Yes. I have even seen a couple of angels and had angels intervene to save me from death. It is not only that I witnessed these angels, but I was taught about angels through the Bible and Churches. I have attended many Churches in my years of life, almost all Christian denominations, and learned that God exists, Jesus existed, and there are such things as angels that visit people in their hour of need. My family members have had angel visits and witnessed angels in human form visit them. Angels come to us in human form so as not to scare us; that is where the shapeshifting occurs. This author believes in the higher beings near us, just a thin dimensional veil away. I would not write about this angel topic if I were not a Godly person. If you read all the stories in this book and think I am not a believer - you are wrong.

I write about Biblical beasts, Nephilim, Giants, Leviathan, and other beasts in Biblical text. In addition, I cover Cryptids, Big Foot, Dogmen, and Skinwalkers, all supernatural beings from another dimension that people have witnessed throughout thousands of years. I discuss these beings to show you that all these supernatural beings exist outside our realm and can travel through time and space as angels do rapidly. Time and space are not obstacles to these beings through wormholes or tunnels – time travel.

The ancient religious texts speak about the Watchers or (fallen angels) in the Book of Enoch, and it was not included in the Bible by King Constantine in and around 325 AD. It was said that these apocryphal Books did not fit with the Churches' beliefs and they would be disruptive to the Christian Church. I believe there are some truths in these books of apocryphal text. The books of Mary, Judas, Enoch, Thomas, Lilith, and Adam and Eve were not accepted in the Christian Bible. I find these books very interesting, especially those of Mary and Enoch. They are said to be written between two hundred BC and three hundred AD. I believe these books could tell us more about Christ and the very beginnings of Christianity. I think all these ancient religious texts are exciting and could reveal information. The books are considered hidden books. In this book, I visualize all the secrets of the ancients. The author keeps an open mind and allows consciousness to help piece together our supernatural world.

Why incorporate all these supernatural beings with angels? This author believes that angels are extraterrestrial, as I explain in this book. Any entity that comes into our realm of Earth from another dimension or planet is extraterrestrial. Then, why do I write about fairies, gnomes, and other monsters? Many humans have seen these creatures I mentioned in this book for thousands of years. Mythology is not made-up of fictional stories; they have some truth to them, like all mythology, like Greek mythology and the philosophers Socrates, Plato, and Aristotle that we study in college. Could these men of knowledge be all wrong? No. The same with mythological creatures like dragons, for instance. They are mentioned in religious texts, and philosophers speak of them in their writings. Why believe some myths and not others?

In our present day, we have mythology surrounding us, as I mentioned in this book, for instance, Big Foot, extraterrestrial aliens, and UFOs. The ancient people saw things they could not explain, like angels, giants, aliens, and giant beasts like dragons and leviathans – mentioned in the Bible. Our human history has been full of mysteries. Life itself is a miracle. We are all supernatural beings with a soul and spiritual energy that makes us immortal and powerful.

This author has seen angels, extraterrestrials, and UFOs with my own eyes and with witnesses. These events made me firmly believe that God's spiritual energy makes anything possible. God created all life, matter, planets, and eleven scientifically proven universes. God can make anything happen in time and space and show us the miracles only He can create.

ABOUT THE AUTHOR

I was born in a small Southern Illinois town in the great Midwest in the late 1940s, at a time when there were no computers and kids like me. I spent most of my time playing outside. We had to use our imaginations to play games and explore the woods and a cardboard box was our best toy. We were a poor blue-collar family that had to think less about money and more about having fun. I had ten brothers and sisters, so we were taught to share. Our family was not associated with any Church, but our mother taught us good morals and to obey the law. My mother was our direct guardian angel, though I am sure she depended greatly on her spiritual strength to raise eleven kids independently. I had teachers tell me I was exceptional and made me feel better. My mother told me I was special because I was born with gray, long sideburns. My brothers and I would visit Churches from time to time and learn some Bible basics.

I graduated from high school on the honor roll and was told my IQ was above average (138), but I did not have the education stressed to me by my parents except for high school level. My brother and I went into the US Army together after high school because the draft took all young men that could not afford college. I went to South Vietnam and fought as a combat platoon sergeant for a year, very nearly missed being killed several times, and that is when I began to consider that I had a guardian angel. I knew at that time that there was something greater than us.

My brothers and I (seven of us real family brothers) played in a band called "Crystal Image" for 45 years. God and His angels gave us a talent that we could share with people to help them enjoy life. If God gives you talents, you are supposed to use them. During that same period, I worked as an electrician, managing small businesses, and as a lead person in an oil refinery. I attended college for those years, finishing five years of Mass Communication schooling in Radio and Television courses.

As mentioned within, the real reason I wrote this book is I have seen mysterious entities like extraterrestrials, UFOs, and angels in real-time. This past year, I wrote a book on the UFO subject and lifetime experiences. I have visited and attended most Christian churches and was even a Catholic. Attending these religious services and even playing rock gospel music in bands at Churches made me ask more questions that Pastors could not answer. My bucket list consisted of writing a spiritual book about our souls and life journeys on earth before we leave for Heaven. My books are intended to share my experiences to enlighten all interested in learning life's mysteries.

Life does not stop here – we are eternal.

AFTERWORD

Go to hangar1publishing.com to learn more about the Author and stay up to date with their newest releases.

www.ingramcontent.com/pod-product-compliance
Lightning Source LLC
Chambersburg PA
CBHW061148120626
46546CB00005B/1973